T0246003

ITALY'S GRANDE TRAVERSATA DELLE ALPI

GTA: THROUGH THE ITALIAN ALPS
FROM THE SWISS BORDER TO THE MEDITERRANEAN

By David Jordan

JUNIPER HOUSE, MURLEY MOSS,
OXENHOLME ROAD, KENDAL, CUMBRIA LA9 7RL
www.cicerone.co.uk

© David Jordan 2023
Second Edition 2023
ISBN: 978 1 78631 040 8
First edition 2005 by Gillian Price
ISBN: 978 1 85284 417 2

Printed in Singapore by KHL Printing on responsibly sourced paper.
A catalogue record for this book is available from the British Library.
All photographs are by the author unless otherwise stated.

Route mapping by Lovell Johns www.lovelljohns.com
Contains OpenStreetMap.org data © OpenStreetMap
contributors, CC-BY-SA. NASA relief data courtesy of ESRI

Updates to this guide

While every effort is made by our authors to ensure the accuracy of guidebooks as they go to print, changes can occur during the lifetime of an edition. Any updates that we know of for this guide will be on the Cicerone website (www.cicerone.co.uk/1040/updates), so please check before planning your trip. We also advise that you check information about such things as transport, accommodation and shops locally. Even rights of way can be altered over time. We are always grateful for information about any discrepancies between a guidebook and the facts on the ground, sent by email to updates@cicerone.co.uk or by post to Cicerone, Juniper House, Murley Moss, Oxenholme Road, Kendal, LA9 7RL.

Register your book: To sign up to receive free updates, special offers and GPX files where available, create a Cicerone account and register your purchase via the 'My Account' tab at www.cicerone.co.uk.

Front cover: Military barracks below Lago Valasco (Stage 43)

CONTENTS

Mountain safety

Every mountain walk has its dangers, and those described in this guidebook are no exception. All who walk or climb in the mountains should recognise this and take responsibility for themselves and their companions along the way. The author and publisher have made every effort to ensure that the information contained in this guide was correct when it went to press, but, except for any liability that cannot be excluded by law, they cannot accept responsibility for any loss, injury or inconvenience sustained by any person using this book.

International distress signal (*emergency only*)
Six blasts on a whistle (and flashes with a torch after dark) spaced evenly for one minute, followed by a minute's pause. Repeat until an answer is received. The response is three signals per minute followed by a minute's pause.

Helicopter rescue: use the following signals to communicate with a helicopter:

Help needed:
raise both arms
above head to
form a 'Y'

Help not needed:
raise one arm
above head, extend
other arm downward

Emergency telephone numbers:
Police 112
Ambulance 118
Fire Brigade 115
Forest firefighting service 1515

The dialling code for Italy is +39.

Mountain rescue can be very expensive – be adequately insured.

ROUTE SUMMARY TABLE

Stage	From	To	Distance (km)	Time (hr/min)	Ascent (m)	Descent (m)	High Point (m)	Low Point (m)	Page
1	Nufenen Pass	Rifugio Margaroli	17.5	7hr	970	1275	2583	1815	37
2	Rifugio Margaroli	Alpe Devero	13.75	5hr	470	1010	2599	1631	42
3	Alpe Devero	Alpe Veglia	13	5hr 30min	955	835	2461	1631	49
4	Alpe Veglia	Varzo	18.75	7hr 45min	820	2035	2179	568	53
5	Varzo	Rifugio San Bernardo	16	7hr	1755	655	2252	568	58
6	Rifugio San Bernardo	Alpe Cheggio	16	6hr 45min	1055	1200	2327	1497	62
7	Alpe Cheggio	Molini	18.75	7hr 15min	985	1985	1550	485	67
8	Molini	Campello Monti	15.75	7hr 15min	1820	990	2037	485	72
9	Campello Monti	Rifugio Alpe Baranca	18.75	8hr 30min	1635	1345	1924	1036	77
10	Rifugio Alpe Baranca	Carcoforo	8.5	4hr	655	950	2239	1304	83
11	Carcoforo	Rima	9.5	4hr 45min	1055	925	2351	1304	87
12	Rima	Rifugio Valle Vogna	15.25	6hr 45min	1220	1270	2324	1112	90
13	Rifugio Valle Vogna	Rifugio Rivetti	14.5	6hr	1250	435	2493	1380	97
14	Rifugio Rivetti	S. San Giovanni	14.5	6hr 15min	600	1755	2201	895	101
15	S. San Giovanni	S. di Oropa	7.25	3hr 30min	590	465	1622	1020	106
16	S. di Oropa	Trovinasse	18	7hr 45min	1450	1180	2318	1180	110
17	Trovinasse	Quincinetto	7	2hr 45min	10	1145	1435	289	116
18	Quincinetto	Fondo	17.5	8hr 30min	1975	1195	2045	295	122
19	Fondo	Piamprato	11.75	5hr 45min	1345	865	2372	1062	127

Stage	From	To	Distance (km)	Time (hr/min)	Ascent (m)	Descent (m)	High Point (m)	Low Point (m)	Page
20	Piamprato	Ronco Canavese	16.5	8hr	1475	2090	2578	946	131
21	Ronco Canavese	Talosio	10	4hr 45min	1180	905	2050	889	136
22	Talosio	San Lorenzo	13	6hr 30min	1370	1545	2175	1042	140
23	San Lorenzo	Ceresole Reale	26	10hr 45min	1935	1465	2011	826	144
24	Ceresole Reale	Pialpetta	12.5	6hr	1115	1550	2641	1050	150
25	Pialpetta	Balme	15	6hr 45min	1605	1195	2498	1050	154
26	Balme	Usseglio	11.5	6hr 30min	1175	1400	2445	1277	157
27	Usseglio	Il Trucco	23	8hr 30min	1430	985	2546	1277	162
28	Il Trucco	Susa	7	2hr 45min	5	1210	1706	494	167
29	Susa	Alpe Toglie	11.75	5hr	1140	85	1564	494	171
30	Alpe Toglie	Usseaux	15.5	6hr 45min	1245	1355	2595	1404	174
31	Usseaux	Balsiglia	19	7hr 45min	1360	1430	2708	1370	179
32	Balsiglia	Ghigo di Prali	16	6hr 15min	845	765	1705	1150	184
33	Ghigo di Prali	Villanova	19	8hr	1210	1425	2451	1231	188
34	Villanova	Rifugio Barbara Lowrie	12.5	5hr 45min	1175	655	2373	1231	192
35	Rifugio Barbara Lowrie	Rifugio Quintino Sella	14	6hr 30min	1440	560	2650	1753	196
36	Rifugio Quintino Sella	Castello	11	4hr	190	1240	2764	1583	201
37	Castello	Rifugio Meleze	14.75	6hr	1040	825	2284	1590	209
38	Rifugio Meleze	Chiappera	15.25	6hr 15min	1000	1160	2804	1622	213

Stage	From	To	Distance (km)	Time (hr/min)	Ascent (m)	Descent (m)	High Point (m)	Low Point (m)	Page
39	Chiappera	Rifugio della Gardetta	17	7hr	1245	555	2437	1622	218
40	Rifugio della Gardetta	Sambuco	19.5	7hr	480	1645	2535	1280	222
41	Sambuco	Strepeis	11	5hr 30min	1140	1035	2243	1132	226
42	Strepeis	Rifugio Malinvern	21.25	9hr	1830	1300	2600	1273	230
43	Rifugio Malinvern	Terme di Valdieri	13.5	5hr 30min	745	1180	2520	1368	235
44	Terme di Valdieri	Rifugio Genova-Figari	14	6hr 15min	1255	635	2538	1368	239
45	Rifugio Genova-Figari	San Giacomo	11.25	4hr 30min	465	1240	2463	1225	244
46	San Giacomo	Trinita	11	4hr 45min	730	865	1572	1001	247
47	Trinita	Palanfrè	10.5	5hr	1105	810	2203	1091	251
48	Palanfrè	Limonetto	10.5	4hr 45min	865	970	2274	1294	254
49	Limonetto	Rifugio Garelli	23.5	9hr 15min	1710	1030	2220	1294	258
50	Rifugio Garelli	Upega	16.25	7hr	1130	1805	2228	1280	262
51	Upega	Monesi di Triora	9	3hr 45min	430	345	1627	1280	267
52	Monesi di Triora	Colle Melosa	20	7hr 45min	1275	1120	2150	1310	270
53	Colle Melosa	Rifugio Gola di Gouta	16.25	7hr	910	1230	1847	1173	275
54	Rifugio Gola di Gouta	Rifugio Alta Via	16.5	5hr 45min	265	955	1213	548	279
55	Rifugio Alta Via	Ventimiglia	12.5	4hr	160	690	548	0	283

Griespass on the Swiss–Italian border (Stage 1)

Turquiose meltwater in the Bacino o Cheggio (Stage 6)

INTRODUCTION

Well-maintained tracks make easy walking (Stage 9)

There is no doubt that this is one of the great alpine treks. Just over 800km, over 57,000m of ascent and descent, trekking across Italy from the Swiss border in the high Alps, all the way to the sea, where you can walk no further. The aficionado of mountaineering peaks will appreciate passing Monte Rosa, Rocciamelone, Rocca la Meja, Monviso and the epic spires of the Argentera. In the course of this great journey, you will pass through no less than five unique alpine regions; the Lepontine Alps, the Pennine Alps, the Graian Alps, the Cottian Alps and the Maritime Alps.

Yet none of these facts will form the memories you are most likely to treasure from this journey. These will be drawn from the smaller things. The things that make the GTA a unique trek, fundamentally different from the multitude of other great trekking opportunities that you could choose in the Alps. When I ask other people about their experience of the western Alps they talk about the Ecrins, the Vanoise or perhaps even the Queyras regions on the French side of the Alps. Few seem genuinely aware of the great diversity and opportunity among the mountains on the Italian side of the watershed that forms the border. Among these mountains life has gone on, quietly, in much the same way as it always has. There are not the big ski resorts, no large hotels, no great promotional campaigns luring in visitors, no commercialisation of culture selling replicas hastily assembled abroad. It is just, quieter.

This is the difference. The Italian side of the alpine chain is just a little bit wilder. A bit less managed. There is a sense that things here are as they always have been, perhaps as they should be. High among the great peaks, prehistoric-looking ibex clash horns, the sound echoing clear across the stillness. Light-footed chamois skip across great slopes of scree. Below in alpine meadows, lop-eared Biellese sheep cluster together, and moving among them, almost hidden, the larger outline of the fierce Maremma sheepdogs, the age-old protection against the all but invisible wolves that still range vast distances through these mountains. The practice of transhumance still sets the rhythm of the seasons here. Great flocks are herded far from valley homes, exploiting alpine meadows as snow recedes. Herders, moving with their flocks, live an unenviably hard existence, bedding down in the most basic *alpe* huts, roofed with great slabs of stone. Tradition is strong here, and with it a sense of history that does more to define the present than in most of our lives.

Travelling through these mountains day after day somehow requires the visitor to be more than just that. Nothing is packaged, presented, translated or sold, at least metaphorically speaking. There is less in terms of the industry of tourism, supporting the traveller and making life easier. Yet that absence is what makes the journey so much more enriching. You need to become a part of the story, to engage with people and the landscape in a way that you don't in so many places, where you remain merely an outsider.

It is a bold start when devising a walking route to title it a Grand Traverse, and yet nothing less would truly capture the essence of this route. The route's founders recognised this. It really is a grand and wonderful journey of exploration and discovery. Indeed, I will be quite surprised at anyone who undertakes this adventure and doesn't fall just a little bit in love with the region, its places, history and people.

THE GTA ROUTE

Devised in the 1970s, the Italian GTA route was inspired to some extent by the success of the French equivalent, which connects Lake Geneva with the coast at Nice, although most now know it only as the southern part of the longer GR5 route. Originally devised to run south to north, the GTA began at Viozene, near Ormea and ended at the unremarkable Molini di Calasca, a route of approximately 633km. The project was as much an economic one as it was a celebration of the mountains. Undoubtedly negotiations were necessary with local and regional groups over the choice of route, and inevitably therefore who or

where benefitted, and where was left out. Rather than a single, clear route, this led to a network of paths, variants and options. While this may be great for exploring an area, in some ways it did little more than add the label of the GTA to existing paths.

After the initial enthusiasm ebbed away, many of the routes were less maintained, and with little promotion the route could have been lost. Its continued existence we owe undoubtedly to the renowned German professor of cultural geography, Werner Bätzing, who has researched the area over several decades and whose two-volume German-language guide books, now in their 8th edition, are unquestionably the definitive work. In the intervening time other authors have also have published guides in Italian and German. The first English-language guide was published by Cicerone in 2005 and written by Gillian Price. I am indebted to both for trusting me with this re-write. A lot has changed however. The route has been extended, most now recognise the GTA as being border to sea, and most also now walk north to south. There is something about starting high in the mountains on a border, and walking south until stopped by the sea. There is still inconsistency, too. A prominent Italian guide has the route bypassing the northern border and finishing at Lake Maggiore. The German-language guides tend to still include a number of variant options. What I have sought to do in this guide is to provide a single continuous route, using what I believe to be the most recognised route from end to end. This is not to discourage venturing off the route,

The beautiful Parco Naturale Valsesia (Stage 8)

indeed I positively encourage it, but to ensure that those with limited time and resources have a clear reference point from which to plan their journey.

On many maps still, while much of the route appears clear, GTA markings can be found in several areas, some far apart and not necessarily connecting sections in the way that you might expect. This is particularly true of the stages in the north (Stages 4–6), south of Susa (Stages 30–34) and around Valle Maira (Stages 38–44). The same happens with regard to markings on the ground. It is important to be aware of this and refer to the guide when needed.

An introduction to this route cannot be made without an acknowledgement to the CAI; the Italian Alpine Club, whose earlier members devised the beginnings of what this route has become, and whose current members and volunteers undertake the regular work of keeping the path identifiable in places where the lush spring and summer vegetation and wildflowers would otherwise disguise it in weeks.

THE SECTIONS AND STAGES

Presented as three sections, north, central and south, the route can be broken down and walked in several trips if that is your preference. The section ends have been chosen to ensure transport in or out of a section is straightforward and details have been given in each section introduction. The sections correspond closely to the areas covered by the newly available 1:25,000 scale map booklets published by National Geographic, making these the easiest choice of mapping to carry. You could also choose to break the route into two sections, in which case Susa is almost exactly 400 kilometres from either end, and with excellent facilities and transport connections this is an obvious choice. For those with the time and resources, undertaking a single continuous 'thru-hike', the section ends are a great place to resupply, take stock, get laundry done and so on. Whatever your approach, the journey is a deeply rewarding experience.

The stages are not necessarily intended to be walked as days. Many are an ideal length, and most have been chosen to connect with limited available accommodation. However, everyone is an individual, we all walk at a different pace and want different things from our day. Some stages can be combined, and some

longer ones you may want to break into two. Accommodation options listed include those available part-way through a stage, and some not far off the route as well as those which correspond with a stage end. Stages don't therefore need to be followed precisely. Indeed, some great accommodation options lie within a stage.

The northern section is divided into 17 stages, the central and southern sections 19 stages. Both the latter sections are about 280km while the first is closer to 240km. Both the north and south sections are very similar in terms of overall climb and fall with around 17,000m of ascent and 19,000m of descent. The central section has a little more with ascent being over 23,000m and descent just under 22,000m. In all this amounts to around 345 hours of walking.

The peaks of Monte Rosa loom large beyond the iron cross of Colle d'Egua (Stage 10)

WEATHER AND WHEN TO GO

The route is best walked between the months of June and September. A typical year can see snow remain on high ground into mid-June, and on the highest passes traces may remain even later. By late September the autumn storms are getting started and rain will be more frequent. Outside of these months accommodation options outside of the villages become severely limited too, as many operators are only open for the summer season.

Trail conditions do vary from year to year, as well as throughout the season. A particularly wet spell can contribute significantly to trail erosion and minor temporary re-routes may be in place as a result.

The middle two weeks in August are when most Italians take their holiday. As a result, trails suddenly become busier and accommodation needs to be booked well in advance. Weekends either side of this can be busy too, especially in areas where vehicle access is easier.

GETTING THERE AND BACK

For many, perhaps hiking a section at a time in a short break from work, time will be of the essence and flying will be the most efficient option to get as far as Milan, which is a logical main connection from which to travel onwards and enables a return fare to be booked. Turin is nearer to much of the trail than Milan, but at the time of writing is only served by one UK airport, whereas Milan is serviced by several airlines from many larger UK and European airports, including low-cost and national carriers. Milan Malpensa (MXP) provides the easiest onward connections, with a direct train from the airport to Milan Central Station taking just fifty-one minutes.

If you are planning a 'thru-hike' of the GTA and will complete the walk in a single season, then it makes sense to separate your outward and return journeys, perhaps leaving the return journey booking until near the end of the trip. If flying outbound, then either Milan or Zurich are valid choices of destination airport and both offer incredible onward train journeys to Airolo from where the Postbus departs to Nufenen Pass. The return journey after reaching Ventimiglia can be made from either Nice or Genoa airports. Nice is an easy one-hour train west, whereas Genoa is around two hours east along the coastline.

If you can afford a more relaxed journey, I would encourage travel by rail, both as the low-carbon option, and as a more satisfying experience. The better sense of distance from home, and the more gradual transition from 'normal life' to your time hiking in the mountains can be much more rewarding. Rail travel in most of Europe is efficient and somewhat cheaper than in the UK. Rail travel in northern Italy is relatively cheap and efficient, and a connection from Milan to Turin takes under two hours direct. All you ever needed to know

Taking the 111 bus to Nufenen Pass (Stage 1)

about planning and booking a long-distance train journey can be found on the website of 'the man in seat sixty-one' (www.seat61.com).

Details of transport to the trailheads is given in the route descriptions.

LOCAL TRANSPORT

Once in Italy, onward train journeys to any of the trail section starts or finishes (or the nearest main town with a station), can be easily booked using either the national carrier website Trenitalia (www.trenitalia.com), or their excellent phone app. Both have an English-language option indicated by a UK flag in the top right of the page. You will need to use Italian place names, however, which is not difficult, for example Milan = Milano,

Turin = Torino. An alternative that can use English-language place names for Italian places is www.italiarail.com. It can be simpler in some ways and can be more effective at finding the cheapest fare, particularly if more than one person is travelling, but do be aware that they charge a booking fee of around €3.50 which can negate any benefit on some journeys. The Trainline website (www.thetrainline.com) and app also now operate in Italy and provide an easy alternative for making bookings.

There are broadly two types of trains in Italy, long-distance and regional. For long-distance trains in Italy an advance reservation will secure the best prices and seats, much like an airline. On regional trains it is not usual to book in advance, rather just turn up and use the ticket machine at the station. They are easy to use and have full instructions in multiple languages. Long-distance train tickets can also be purchased from ticket machines prior to the journey, but the price is likely to be significantly higher than booking in advance. For either train type, just remember that if you have a physical ticket, purchased from a machine or a ticket office, you must get it validated **before** you get on the train. This can be done by 'punching' the ticket briefly into a machine, usually on the platform or nearby.

The final section of your journey to or from some trail sections will be by bus. Buses in Italy tend to be regionally based and there have been few attempts at bringing together information and timetables at a national level. That said, you don't need it. Almost every valley

that you may want to get in or out of will have a bus, even if it only runs a couple of times a day. It is easy to turn up, find a bus stop, check the provided timetable and pay the driver when you board the bus. In towns and cities however, be aware that tickets should be purchased before boarding, usually at the nearest *tabac* (tobacconist/newsagent). However, if you are really keen to try to establish bus routes and times in advance, the website Rome to Rio (www.rome2rio.com) does an amazing job of scouring the furthest corners of the internet for published information on almost every imaginable form of travel, and then presenting it to you as a simple set of options. While occasionally the algorithms may find and present some out-of-date information, it does do an incredible job 99 per cent of the time.

The GTA route enables some far-reaching views (Stage 53)

HIKING THE GTA

Hiking the GTA is within reach of any average, reasonably fit walker. If you start just a little out of shape, you will not finish so. The terrain is such that the alpine ridges lie for the most part east to west. The trail runs primarily north to south, so it is inevitable that a good deal of climb and fall is experienced. Indeed, a typical day's hiking will include a long climb, often as much as one thousand metres, to an alpine pass, followed by a descent to a *posto tappa* in a small hamlet in an upper valley, or on occasion several climbs and descents to end at a mountain *rifugio*. No technical skills are required. From time to time an exposed or eroded section may be protected with the provision of a rope or chain to assist you. Steep ground is encountered in places, and you will become used to taking care with your footing, while simultaneously gazing at the astounding views. In a couple of places there are steep sections that are fine with care in good weather, but risky in poor and wet weather. Where these occur there are alternative paths that, while they may add a little to the day's overall effort and distance, undoubtedly offer a wiser choice than taking any unnecessary risks.

Trail surfaces vary wildly from short sections of tarmac, to barely there tracks across scree or boulders, often navigated primarily with the help of small cairns and sporadic trail markings. In between are shepherd tracks, migration routes, pilgrimage routes, mountain paths broad and narrow, ancient coffin routes, military roads and perhaps one of the delights of this trail over many others, the *mulattiera*. These are what they sound like, ancient trade routes for pack mules that wind their way through the mountains, sometimes steep, but often created with switchbacks that eased the climb or descent for the laden mule (or hiker)! These typically cobbled routes can be found regularly along the trail, in various states of use or disrepair. Often deep in forests or crossing high mountain passes, these trails give a fascinating insight into the nature of the connections between places that long pre-date the motorcar, aeroplane, or train. They also hint at a long history of walking on these routes, and of the people whose footsteps you now follow.

WAYMARKING AND MAPS

The trail is waymarked with a combination of signs on posts, walls, trees and buildings. These are red and white, state the next prominent place on route, and the approximate hours/minutes of walking to reach it. Many will also carry a route number, reflecting the fact that most major walking routes in Italy are numbered in a similar way to the road system in the UK. There will also be red and white blazes on rocks and cairns to guide the walker in difficult conditions. It is important to remember that red and white signs and blazes mark

The path is vague across Pian Madoro so watch for sporadic blazes on rocks (Stage 48)

almost all walking routes in Italy, not just the GTA, and that the GTA is made up of hundreds of connecting footpaths that pre-existed even the concept of a GTA. Some such signs will explicitly state 'GTA', but many will not, and where there are a number of options it is useful to refer to a map, GPS device or this guidebook, all of which will help to keep you on the right track. On occasion you will also see apparently conflicting signs for the GTA. This arises because the GTA was not originally conceived as a single, definitive route, but a network of options that enabled exploring the region as well as getting from end to end.

The exception to the norm is in the Parc Nationale Gran Paradiso, where the trail touches on the corner of the Aosta Valley. Here yellow markers are used to signify footpaths, and these will usually be marked specifically with 'GTA'.

The route is not generally difficult to follow, but signs can be damaged or moved, blazes can become obscured by undergrowth, and it is easy to lose concentration and follow the 'obvious' track ahead, when the path you wanted took a smaller junction to one side of the path you are on. A useful practice is to always look ahead a little on the map and in the guide to see what is coming up next, how the terrain might change, or whether you pass buildings, a stream or other useful markers. If what happens on the ground is not what you were expecting, stop and double check. Even after many years of hiking, I will admit to making at least one such error on every trip, usually blamed on a stunning view, interesting build-ing, or fascinating plant. However, the quicker a navigational error is spotted, the easier it is corrected.

Mapping for the GTA has become considerably easier with the recent publication by National Geographic of the final of their three map book-lets for the GTA; North, Central and South. Before this as many as eleven maps were needed to cover the route, even at 1:50,000 scale. It is important to note, however, that these were pro-duced in collaboration with writers of a German-language guidebook to the route. As such, they follow or include several route variants and options that do not appear in this book. In particu-lar a small section of this route (Stages 51 and 52) is not wholly covered by the boundaries of the National Geographic southern booklet. The Blu Edzioni Imperia 1:50k is a good alter-native here. That said, the booklet for-mat, printed at a scale of 1:25,000, on waterproof paper, make them by far the best paper map option now avail-able for most of the route.

Italy has no national cartographic organisation and historically maps for the Piedmont region were produced by the IGC (Institute Geographico Centrale), a company based in Turin. These were not renowned for their accuracy. In recent years several map-ping organisations have sprung up with decent offerings and mapping options are suggested at the intro-duction of each stage. In addition to hard-copy maps, it is useful to carry either a dedicated GPS device, or a GPS mobile phone app, to which you can upload the provided GPX tracks to locate the route on a digital map.

ACCOMMODATION

Overnight stays on the GTA provide some of the richest experiences of the trail. They can range from the simplest of self-catered huts in the *bivaccos*, some of which are best considered as emergency shelters only, to the really quite luxurious small boutique hotels in a handful of places. Increasingly hikers have the ability to choose, with the options increasing year by year. Most however, are the small vil-lage *posto tappa*, literally a 'stopping place' usually a family owned and run bar, restaurant and lodging that is the hub of village life. You will also see the term *agriturismo*. These are usu-ally farms or local producers of dairy products closely linked to a farm, that open up their homes to visitors. These can be rewarding experiences, with hosts keen to share information and stories about the local area and his-tory. The small hotels, known as *alber-gos* in Italy are usually family owned too, and can be found in many of the larger villages where you are likely to have several options to choose from.

In the more rugged mountainous stretches, you will stay in a *rifugio*. These are akin to the mountain ref-uges found all over the Alps, with dor-mitories or shared rooms. These are usually run by the national mountain

Usseaux main square (Stage 30)

club, in this case the Club Alpino Italiano (CAI), although in Italy there are also many privately owned refuges. Discounts are offered to members, and also to members of other national clubs such as the British Mountaineering Council (BMC), so if you're not already, do consider becoming a member. They also provide one of the best travel insurance policies for hikers and trekkers.

Wild camping is prohibited in Italy. That said, in practice it is a similar situation to England, where no one will bother you provided you are sensible about where and when you pitch, and you scrupulously ensure you follow leave no trace principles. Always aim to camp well away from farms and villages, avoid livestock, and protect water sources. Always ask first at a *rifugio*. Many hosts will

be happy to let you camp nearby and will usually be happy to charge for a meal only. It is perfectly possible to take a tent and camp some or all of the way, indeed I have come across people who have. But I would encourage you to use accommodation providers for at least some nights. Not only does it give you a much richer experience of the trail, but it is also a valuable source of income for these small mountain communities.

Booking far in advance isn't usually necessary outside of peak season (the middle two weeks of August in Italy, when it seems everyone is on holiday). However, it is courteous to telephone the night before and reserve, especially if you want dinner, so the host can be prepared. Most accommodation providers will be happy to telephone ahead for you if you ask. This is common practice in the mountains where mobile signal is often unreliable. Do consider booking further ahead, however, in peak season and at weekends, especially where the accommodation you want is within walking distance of a trailhead, or likely to be popular, for example Rifugio della Gardetta in Stage 39.

Accommodation costs of course vary but expect to pay on average around €50–60 for *mezza pensione* (half board) at most providers, with a little more in hotels.

FOOD AND DRINK

Food and drink along the trail is one of the reasons for undertaking this particular hike. It is no surprise to learn that this region saw the birth of the Slow Food Movement. A movement that celebrates diversity, it places the richness and quality of the food above else. Production, harvest, transport, storage, preparation and serving are all managed with the protection of quality and flavour in mind. Meals, or the preparation of them, are not to be rushed. Mealtimes are a social occasion and if you find yourself at such a meal on this adventure (and you will), eat slowly, talk a lot, try new things, get to know your companions and savour the wine – it will almost certainly be among the best you have tasted for this is the home of the Nebbiolo grape, famed for wines such as Barolo and Barbaresco.

Cena (dinner) is usually around *setta e mezza* (seven thirty) or later. Meals in Italy are generally started with *antipasti*, a starter that can be enormously varied and often a regional speciality. Next comes your *primo piatto/corso*, often a pasta dish, followed by *secondi piatto/corso*, normally a form of meat with vegetables, followed by dessert (or *dolce*), again a rich variety of local and regional specialities can be served, and where you have a range of choices it is always worth asking, '*Qual'é la vostra specialità?*', what is the local speciality?

Most Italians take great pride in the sourcing and presentation of their food and will go to great lengths to find and prepare ingredients in a way that maximises flavour. Asking about the ingredients and complementing your hosts on the food can generate an enormous amount of goodwill and is a great way to 'break the ice' and start conversations, even with limited Italian. '*Il cibo è delizioso*' will always generate a smile!

Breakfast (*colazione*) in Italy is often more limited. Italians eat dinner late, so breakfast is usually small, sweet and brief. Coffee, usually cappuccino or latte, is often served in a bowl, accompanied by small sweet baked goods such as a slice of cake, croissant or brioche with jam or honey, and a biscuit. In a *rifugio*, fresh goods are very limited. Most supplies are delivered by helicopter or mule, a few times in a season, so you will see the small, packet mini toasts too.

If you are used to a little more before a day's walking, it is worth carrying a few supplies of your own.

WHAT TO TAKE

With accommodation and meals available daily, and other supplies available at various places along the trail, it is not necessary to carry a large backpack. Indeed, this is one of the pleasures of such a route, you really can travel light. Comfortable footwear and protection from the rain is of course essential, and even a smaller rucksack should be well-fitting and have a waistbelt, but a few other items will make your journey more comfortable too. Choices over what to wear and carry are quite personal but the following list should be a good guide or checklist of things to think about.

Rucksack – around 40 litres is usually enough. A waistbelt reduces pulling on your shoulders and accessible belt pockets can be useful. Take an integrated or additional waterproof cover, with dry bags inside, and a selection of resealable freezer-type bags are useful too.

Footwear – comfort and grip are most important. Boots should be lightweight, well-fitting and already broken in. Trail shoes are becoming more popular but are less durable.

Waterproof jacket and trousers – also protect against wind. Try to find waterproofs that are more breathable or have venting you can unzip so they are not too sweaty.

Insulation – in the form of a fleece or synthetic top or jacket (down is not a good choice in this climate as it is too vulnerable to dampness, when it loses its loft).

Warm hat and gloves (or mitts) – In the summer this can seem like overkill, but you will be amazed how quickly it can turn cold in the mountains, especially if you are also wet. Covering your extremities is the quickest way of regulating your temperature. Mitts are more effective than gloves, but of course you lose dexterity.

Sun hat and gloves – the sun at altitude can be intense and a sun hat of whatever form is essential. But gloves, really? It is personal choice, but if you are not used to using trekking poles all day, you will find your hands (especially between your thumb and forefinger) can get really burned. Consider fingerless sun gloves, or a top with thumb loops that can pull down to protect the backs of your hands.

Sunglasses and sunscreen – are essential to protect from the high UV rays.

Insect repellent – is useful in some areas to keep biting insects at bay. Most of the time you won't need it, but when you do, you'll be glad of it.

Hiking clothes – should be lightweight and loose. Merino wool or synthetics are best for drying quickly, and minimising odours. Avoid cotton and denim entirely.

Evening wear – a single set of evening clothes is usually sufficient.

Try to ensure these are lightweight and not bulky. Lightweight alternative footwear such as sandals are also useful. (A *rifugio* will usually provide slip-on sandals or similar.)

Trekking poles – these are highly recommended. Used properly, they help to spread the effort across your body on a climb, but also protect your knees in descent. Few people who try them out ever return to hiking without them. There's little doubt they will extend the number of years you will be hiking for!

Sheet sleeping bag or liner – required in most huts where you will be provided with a blanket and pillow but will be expected to use your own sheet/liner.

Torch – can be small and lightweight. A headtorch is particularly useful. Even if you don't expect to be late off the hill, emergencies can happen, and it can make finding the toilet at night in unfamiliar accommodation much easier.

First aid kit – Only needs to be minimal, but the ability to deal with blisters, stomach bugs, headaches, cuts and grazes and so on, is essential.

Water bottle – ideally be capable of carrying two litres of water. A solid bottle and a soft bottle that can be rolled or folded is an ideal combination.

Whistle – always have one for emergencies even if you never plan to use it. Many rucksacks now come with an integral one.

European plug/converter – no doubt you will want to charge a phone as a minimum, possibly a rechargeable torch, camera, GPS device and more. A two-pin USB wall charger is

Wildflower meadow outside Chiappera (Stage 38)

a good investment. One with UK/Euro interchangeable ends enables you to use it at the airport as well as while away.

Maps – while GPS and phone apps have become the first source of navigation for many, a paper back up is invaluable, and often carries more detail than digital mapping.

Compass – no great technical skill is required but is useful to be able to confirm that you are heading west if that is what the route description indicates.

PREPARATION AND SAFETY

While the route is not technical, much of it is relatively remote and mobile phone signal cannot be relied upon, sometimes for several days at a time. Personal locator beacon devices are now widely available and cheaper than ever before, and these can be useful if it is reassuring for someone at home to be able to track your progress.

Many high passes are crossed and some of these are steep and rugged, requiring surefootedness. There are some exposed areas too, although these are generally protected by the provision of chains, fixed cable or ropes as a handrail and for confidence. Nonetheless there are some sections that are vulnerable to erosion and are considerably more dangerous when the weather is wet. In these cases, there is always a way around a difficult section, even if it means

increasing your hiking distance and altering your plans. It is always better to err on the side of caution.

It goes without saying that increasing your fitness, your leg strength and improving your foot placement before you leave home will go a long way to increasing your enjoyment of the hike. Fortunately, there is no better way to get hill fit, than to walk in the hills, and that is never a chore.

LANGUAGE

It is usual that in most parts of Europe the hiker can get away with very little understanding of languages other than English. While a great deal can be communicated with a little comical mime and gestures, here more than most parts of Europe a little effort to learn a few basic words and phrases will help enormously, not only in gaining access to the things you need along the way, but also in generating smiles, goodwill and laughter. These are the things that will create opportunities and wonderful memories of the journey. In this part of Italy, it is not unusual to meet people who speak no English at all, even at accommodation providers, and an effort to speak a few words in Italian is always appreciated.

Included at Appendix A is a brief glossary of words and phrases you may find useful, but with so many resources now available for free on the internet, it is worth doing some additional learning, perhaps through

Alpe Buscagna superiore (Stage 3)

YouTube videos or the excellent range of language-learning apps for mobile phones and tablets. A small phrasebook with a basic dictionary included is an invaluable resource to carry, too.

ITALY'S WESTERN ALPS

When most people think of the lower end of the great arc of the Alps, they think of the areas south of Chamonix in France; in particular the Vanoise national park and the Ecrins, perhaps the Dauphine Alps, the Mercantour or Provence. Few immediately think of Italy beyond the Aosta valley. Yet Piedmont (or Piemonte) literally means 'foot of the mountains'.

It may come as a surprise to many that during the course of this walk you will cross parts of the Lepontine Alps, the Pennine Alps, the Graian Alps, the Cottian Alps and the Maritime Alps. North-western Italy is mountainous. In the area south of Aosta in particular, the mountain ridges tend to run broadly east to west in orientation, so the amount of ascent and descent encountered is significant. The higher passes are over 2500m in height and typically accommodation is closer to 1000m, so it is easy to see that the amount of daily climb is significant.

As you walk you come to recognise that each area has its own unique character. In the north, once the glaciers and moraine of Switzerland are left behind, the valleys tend to run southward, steep sides are dense with undergrowth, paths seem to defy gravity and the walker passes in and out of the light at every turn. Crossing the Alpe Devero and Alpe Veglia National Park you feel almost that you are back in Switzerland, with gorgeous turquoise lakes and towering peaks. Moving down through Valles Anzasca and Sesia the view of Monte Rosa dominates from the passes and high points. Touching on the Aosta Valley you cross the corner of the Parc Gran Paradiso to reach Lago di Ceresole, then turning more definitively southwards, Monte Viso begins to come into view. In many ways the south is perhaps the biggest surprise, for here you enter the Argentera and could be forgiven for thinking you were on the edge of the Dolomites. Next the colossal views around Colle di Tenda, from where you skip back and forth across the border in the final turn south towards the Mediterranean. While the altitudes inevitably diminish towards

the end of the walk, you are more than content with that after close to 60,000m of climb and descent, yet the route resolutely follows the high ground to the last, descending off the final ridge by sea cliff, with only a short walk to the beach and the sea.

HISTORY

Mountains are often of strategic importance in history, usually as barriers, defences against, or impediments to territorial ambition. Passes therefore, are commonly fought over, protected, coveted and utilised, as much for trade as for military purposes. Inevitably then, mountains wear the scars of history, much more so than other landforms. The mountain borders of Piedmont are no different. The

The trail descends to the sea at Ventimiglia (Stage 55)

remains of minor fortifications are present up and down the passes of the region, but few are as impressive as the forts at Fenestrelle, the largest alpine fortification in Europe, dating from as early as 1690 and at times referred to as the great wall of Europe.

A great deal of former military roads live on as tracks throughout these mountains, and it is not unusual to find references to their importance during World War 1 and 2. But of course, most date to well before this time and many will have origins in the expansion, and defence, of the Roman Empire. The story of these mountains is not only one of military history. Trade too has played a major role. As routes have opened or become un-passable, this has shaped the history and fortunes of people in the area. Few examples illustrate this as well as the effect of the Monviso tunnel, one of the oldest long tunnels in Europe dating back to the Renaissance. It was a significant trade route for around 120 years until changes in political allegiances led the Duke of Savoy to shut it down to ensure that frequented trade routes favoured valleys in his lands further north.

In the northern stages in particular you will encounter many stories of the Waldensians, a protestant group persecuted throughout the centuries as a religious minority, who at various times populated these valleys, fled and returned to fight for their rights. They left behind a wealth of culture, architecture and stories. Several opportunities arise on the journey to learn more about their plight, particularly at the excellent museum on the way into Alagna Valsesia (Stage 12), but also in the tiny museum in Balsiglia (Stage 31) where they fought a heroic battle, outnumbered yet managed a miraculous escape.

So much that is of interest in these mountains however, is not of the big events that shape history, but the stories that are passed through the generations, the cultural aspects that survive and find their way into the architecture, the practices, the homes and lives of ordinary people. It would be hard to walk this route and not come away with an impression of a hardy, resilient yet almost unfailingly welcoming and friendly people, who are deeply rooted in their sense of place.

PLANTS AND FLOWERS

Not everyone will be able to name wildflowers as they pass by, but names are not important. Most people who enjoy the mountains will appreciate diversity of plant life, and welcome the rich profusion of colour that flowering plants provide. Just as with trees, where most of us know a handful of key species, but may not be sure of the precise differences between say, a White and a Noble fir tree. However, that does not detract from the pleasure of the smell of moist pine needles on those first cool days of autumn as you tread gently on their soft, quiet carpet.

Goats are inquisitive trail companions (Stage 4)

The western Italian alpine chain is rich in biodiversity. Traditional, low-intensity methods of farming contribute to this and there are likely to be a few places where you will walk, at times near wade, through enormous meadow basins, knee-deep in grasses and wildflowers of every description. It is an explosion of colour and smell that many of us rarely see. It is a reminder of much that has been lost in other areas, and of how important it is.

However, if you are keen to begin to put names to the plants you see, then Gillian Price's brilliant little book on alpine wildflowers weighs almost nothing and can be purchased here: https://www.cicerone.co.uk/alpine-flowers.

WILDLIFE

Of course, great diversity in plant life is the cornerstone for thriving biodiversity in wildlife too. Here where nature still dominates the landscape rather than humans, crossing alpine meadows means every step sees an explosion of crickets, moths, aphids, butterflies and beetles. Was this how Britain's countryside was before herbicides, pesticides, mechanisation and intensive agriculture?

Here where they have the space to thrive, you can watch the fascinating behaviour of the ever-curious marmots. Mice and voles, too, provide food for birds of prey. Hawks, buzzards, even an eagle or an owl are birds you could see here. Below on the slopes the majestic-looking ibex prefer the advantage of high ground and will often appear as a silhouette on the skyline. Chamois on the other hand, like the scree slopes and upper meadows, where they can see far and move quickly. Then there are the deer, at least three varieties, that prefer the woodlands, the forest and the scrub. Concealment is their strategy for safety.

Perhaps what strikes the visitor most is not the presence of one or two key species, but that this is a rich, diverse, healthy ecosystem. To move among it and spend time quietly observing feels a real privilege.

HOW TO USE THIS GUIDE

The route described is north-south in direction and structured to enable three walks of around three weeks. Stage lengths take into account the terrain, the interest and the available accommodation. These are a guide only and are by no means the only way to walk the route. In a couple of places long stages could be shortened by the use of public transport, in particular where an unavoidable road walk is necessary, where there is little of interest. On one occasion the use of a chairlift enables the walker to access a beautiful area that would otherwise be missed. There is much of interest both on the route, and at stage ends. If you have the time then the route is just a framework within which to explore.

At the beginning of each section an introduction is provided with all of the information necessary to access, or leave, the section start and end points. An overview map gives you a high-level view of the area covered, and summary statistics for the section's overall distance, ascent and so on. You will also find a summary description of the highlights of the section.

In each individual stage you will find a map. These are at 1:100k scale and are a useful reference, but are not intended to replace a topographical map. A route profile is also given which shows the main ups and downs, and key waypoints. A summary of the key information for the stage then follows, with stage start and end points, the distance, ascent, descent and approximate time. The times should be taken as a rough guide and do not include time spent stopped, taking photographs, having lunch and so on. That said, any reasonably fit walker should be able to match these times, and some may find they are quicker. Use them as a benchmark and monitor your own times in the first few days and you will quickly get an idea of whether you are, on average, walking ahead or behind the listed timings. This will then help you to plan ahead. Remember that you will need to allow extra time if the weather is wet, or if paths have become overgrown in some areas.

Before each detailed route description, an outline of the stage is given with any highlights or points to be aware of. Then follows the detailed route description. Key waypoints

Laghi d'Orgials (Stage 42)

are also featured on the stage map where relevant with the height stated. References to 'left' or 'right' in the description are based on the direction of travel. Points of the compass are given where it is useful to add clarity where it is needed and are approximate, such as 'south-west'. No knowledge of compass use is required beyond understanding the direction it is pointing. Always have one in your pocket. A quick glance can confirm your direction and save hours of back-tracking.

Accommodation details are provided at the end of each stage. If a particular accommodation provider is just in the start of the next stage then it is included in the previous one for ease as it is in the immediate vicinity of that stage end. Each entry indicates the type of accommodation provided where known (such as dormitory or double rooms). 'Mixed rooms' refers to rooms typically of four to six beds where, if it is quiet, you may get a room to yourself, otherwise you are likely to be sharing. Addresses are given, and all listed accommodation is marked on the maps. Telephone numbers are given in preference to email addresses as many small providers don't use email. In the Italian Alps the accepted method of booking is to telephone. '*Un letto e una cena per una notte domani, per favore*', literally, a bed and dinner for one night tomorrow please and your name (*nome*), is all you really need.

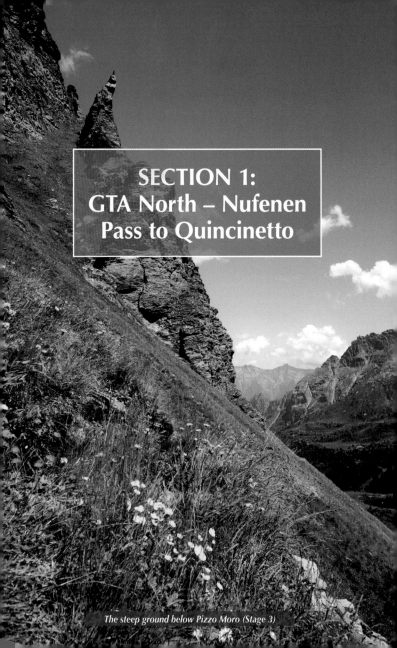

SECTION 1:
GTA North – Nufenen
Pass to Quincinetto

The steep ground below Pizzo Moro (Stage 3)

SECTION 1:
GTA North – Nufenen Pass
to Quincinetto

Distance	242.75km
Ascent	17,295m
Descent	19,455m
Maps	IGC Nos 11, 10 & 9, 1/50k; NatGeo GTA 1 Nord 1/25k
Stages	17

Overview

The northern section of the route covers 17 stages commencing at the top of the Nufenen Pass, close to the Italian–Swiss border at Griespass, all the way to Quincinetto on the south-east corner of the Aosta Valley. From the heart of the Lepontine Alps, the route descends through a region of lakes in the Val Formazza before entering the protected Alpe Devero and Alpe Veglia (the oldest regional park in Italy) areas. The path crosses the Val Divedro at Varzo, then keeps south across Val Antrona and into the Pennine Alps with Valle Anzasca at Molini di Calasca, where the original GTA route (walked south to north) finished. The route then bears west through the Valsesia parks to Alagna, a showcase of Waldensian history, culture and building, leaving by the Val Vogna from where spectacular views of Monte Rosa can be found. Touching momentarily on the corner of the Aosta Valley, the section completes at Quincinetto, a small town just south of Pont Saint Martin.

To Nufenen Pass

Getting to the start of the GTA is straightforward. The route commences from the top of Nufenen Pass, at 2478m the highest paved pass in Switzerland. The pass links the cantons of Valais and Ticino, between Ulrichen and Airolo. From the pass it is about a 2hr walk to the

Swiss–Italian border at Griespass (on some maps/signs referred to as Passo del Gries), at an altitude of 2487m.

From Milan Central Station, take the train north via Lugano or Bellinzona to Airolo, taking around 3hr 30min.

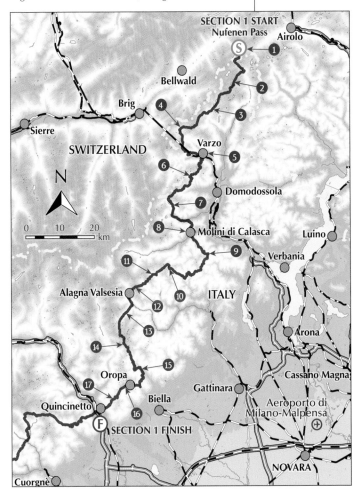

From Zurich Station, take the train south, it's just 2hr directly to Airolo. Booking can be made via SBB, the Swiss National transport provider. Downloading the app for booking and e-tickets is simple and highly recommended.

Ristorante Hotel Des Alpes opposite Airolo station is convenient for an overnight stay if required. Hotel Des Alpes, via Stazione no. 3 – 6780 Airolo CH Ticino, info@ hoteldesalpes-airolo.ch, +41 0 91 869 1722.

From Airolo, take the post bus (111) to Nufenen Passhöhe. Buses run four times a day. Tickets can be purchased on the bus, in advance from the *tabac* and newsagent at Airolo Station or via the SBB app.

If you wish to be walking before the first bus up to the pass in the morning, you can travel up the previous afternoon, alighting from the bus one stop earlier at Alpe di Cruina and walking in via the Val Corno where hut accommodation is available at Capanna Corno Gries (2338m). Continuing up Val Corno the following morning, the path will transect with the main route part-way between Nufenen Pass and the Italian–Swiss border at Griespass.

From Quincinetto
Quincinetto no longer has a railway station, so take bus 265 from Largo Europa (opposite the petrol station) to Pont Saint Martin. Bus tickets can be purchased in advance from the stationary shop round the corner on Via Stazione. From there the train to Milan Central takes around 2hr 20min, or to Turin (Porta Nuova) around 1hr 10min.

STAGE 1
Nufenen Pass to Rifugio Margaroli

Start	Nufenen Pass (2478m)
Finish	Rifugio Margaroli (2194m)
Distance	17.5km
Ascent	970m
Descent	1275m
Time	7hr

Standing at Nufenen Pass the whole adventure is ahead of you. From here you will walk until you can walk no more when you reach the Mediterranean Sea at Ventimiglia. Whether you do that in a continuous 'thru-hike', or as a 'section-hiker' in stages, the experience is no less rewarding. The initial stage sees you cross to the Italian–Swiss border at Griespass, then descend, steeply at times, interspersed by restful and inviting meadow strolls alongside burbling brooks where the temptation is to linger. Passing the turquoise Lago di Morasco, you have an option to descend into Riale for a visit, supplies or rest, before commencing the gradual climb to the first big pass of the route at Passo di Nefelgiu. The descent from here just takes a little care as sections are prone to erosion along the *torrente* that descends into Lago di Vannino, where the hospitality of Rifugio Margaroli awaits the weary trekker.

Leaving **Nufenen Passhöhe** (2478m), cross the car park from the restaurant and climb the small knoll to the right of an old hut, to gain a view of the Gries Glacier and the reservoir in front. Descend ahead, following the small path down to the lower road corner and junction with the reservoir service road. Ascend the service road south, to a side track left to shortcut a road hairpin. Take this and when you reach the next section of road cross and ascend track steps to reach a hut at the base of the wind turbines. From here a red/white trail marking shows your path climbing to the left of the hut. Continue to the left of the dam high on a narrow path around the reservoir.

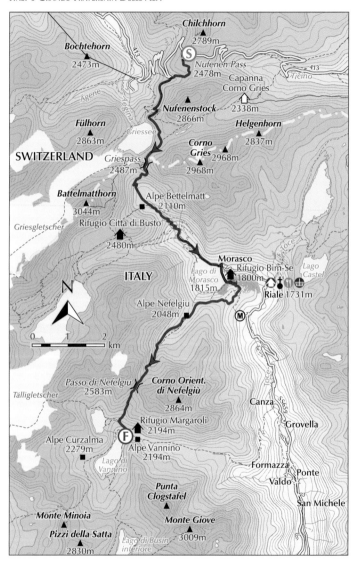

Chilchhorn
2789m

Bochtehorn
2473m

S

Nufenen Pass
2478m

Capanna
Corno Gries
2338m

Nufenenstock
2866m

Helgenhorn
2837m

Fülhorn
2863m

Griessee

SWITZERLAND

Corno
Gries
2968m

Griespass
2487m

Corno
Gries
2968m

Battelmatthorn
3044m

Alpe Bettelmatt
2110m

Griesgletscher

Rifugio Citta di Busto
2480m

Morasco

Rifugio Bim-Se
1800m

Lago
Castel

Lago di
Morasco
1815m

ITALY

Riale 1731m

N

Alpe Nefelgiu
2048m

M

0   1   2
km

Passo di Nefelgiu
2583m

Tälligletscher

Corno Orient.
di Nefelgiù

2864m

Canza

Rifugio Margaroli
2194m

Grovella

Alpe Curzalma
2279m

F

Alpe Vannino
2194m

Formazza

Lago di
Vannino

Ponte
Valdo

San Michele

Punta
Clogstafel

Monte Minoia

Monte Giove
3009m

Pizzi della Satta
2830m

Lago di Busin
interiore

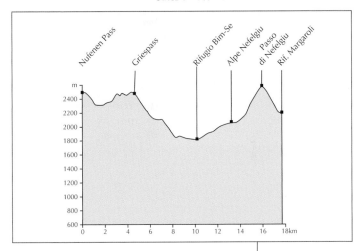

Follow this ahead as the Val Corno track joins on your left and continue on a clear path to Griespass.

Descending from the **Griespass** (2487m), take the trail south (route G00 and marked Via Alpina). It is

Standing at Griespass, with 800km of mountains ahead

sufficiently steep that the path makes good use of switch-backs before traversing south-west, across the head of the valley and two tributary streams of the Rio Gries. Then turn south-east for around 2km, joining the track that leads from Alpe Bettelmatt.

BATTELMATTHORN SUMMIT 3044M

In good weather only, a tempting side excursion from Griespass can be taken to summit the 3044m Battelmatthorn for views west across the Griesgletscher. Leave the pass south-west, then south before a side trail west, just before a high point at 2674m leads to the summit. Returning to the junction, turn S once more, over the high point and descend towards Rifugio Citta di Busto 2480m, then north-east to re-join the GTA at Alpe Bettemmatt.

One of the delights of this journey is the variety of cheeses found on route, unique to the individual valleys or farms. One such is the **Bettelmatt**, with the name believed to date from the 13th century, a semi-cooked cheese made from raw whole cow's milk from Italian brown cows and seasoned for a minimum of 2 months. The aroma of this cheese is closely linked to the mix of herbs and flowers, including the Mutellina herb, characteristic of these pastures.

Follow the track south-east for 0.5km then fork right, on a marked path before crossing to the south side of the Rio Gries at the waterfall. After descending a series of switchbacks, the path levels momentarily then crossing a small stone bridge, the path broadens and climbs gently to the service road and joins a vehicle track once again beyond a hut, continuing south-east along the shore of **Lago di Morasco**.

Unless you plan to go into Riale (1731m) turn right, south and cross over the reservoir wall then left uphill and keep left at the first junction, past a concrete structure marked with a red and white trail blaze. Continue to follow the track up gravelly switchbacks, and along a level stretch with views back across Lago di Morasco.

After a further brief climb the path broadens, reaching a well-marked track junction beside a large pile of quarried stone blocks. Turn right here signed to Lago di Vannino. Passing a small abandoned tunnel on your right, ignore further track junctions and keep ahead on this broad easy-to-follow track.

As you climb now towards Passo di Nefelgiu keep south-west as far as **Alpe Nefelgiu**. Crossing behind the huts and then across the stream, ensure you keep to the north-west bank initially, then the marked route on the ground meanders back and forth across the remains of the stream once up at scree level. Climbing steadily across boulders and scree reach **Passo di Nefelgiu** (2583m). Continue ahead descending steadily along the right flank of the valley through an area prone to erosion and landslides. If you need water, collect it at scree level as anything below is heavily cattle grazed. Multiple markings are confusing but keep right for least problems with erosion. As you descend, over your right shoulder the Punta del Ghiacciaio di Ban (2975m) looms large, while ahead the 2903m peak of Punta del Forno is no

Griesee dam with Gries Glacier beyond

more than a promontory on a ridge that rises to the NE, capped by the snow-topped peak of Punta d'Arbola Ofenhorn (3235m). Almost between the Lakes the trail turns SE once more for around 1km to **Alpe Vannino** and **Rifugio Margaroli** (2194m).

FACILITIES INFORMATION FOR STAGE 1

Accommodation
Rifugio Citta di Busto, dormitory, Località Piano dei Camosci, Formazza (VB), +39 0324 63092

Rifugio BIM-SE, mixed rooms, SS659, 28863 Formazza, (VB), +39 339 5959 3393

Rifugio Margaroli, Località Vannino, 28863 Formazza (VB), +39 0324 63155, +39 327 019 7444

Amenities
Basic shop and a good restaurant in Riale.

Transport
There are no public transport options on route. However, exit from Riale is possible if a ride or taxi can be found to Valdo, where the Comazzibus number 4 runs, four times a day, to Domodossola and onward connections by train.

STAGE 2
Rifugio Margaroli to Alpe Devero

Start	Rifugio Margaroli (2194m)
Finish	Alpe Devero (1631m)
Distance	13.75km
Ascent	470m
Descent	1010m
Time	5hr

A straightforward climb from the Rifugio, followed by a long and mostly gentle descent through the high valley pasture of Alpe Forne Inferiore and onward, descending via a *mulattiera* into a gorgeous lower valley to the picturesque hamlet of Crampiolo where refreshments and local produce can be purchased. From there it is a pleasant stroll to the plain of Alpe Devero.

From **Rifugio Margaroli** retrace your steps a short way to take the path (marked G99, in common with the Via Alpina and the Sentiero Italia) around the far side of **Lago di Vannino**. The path climbs gradually above and away from the lake shore to meet the *torrente* below **Alpe Curzalma** (2279m), where you cross an ingenious bridge made from old pipes. Bear left here initially and follow the red/white trail blazes over rock and scree, contouring gradually west below Punta della Scatta (2720m) then climbing to the pass and **Bivacco E. Conti** at Scatta Minoia (2599m).

Leaving the pass follow the contour right before switchbacks guide you down and past Lago della Satta (2435m). Proceed past a *baita* or hut on your left and cross

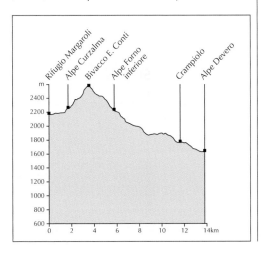

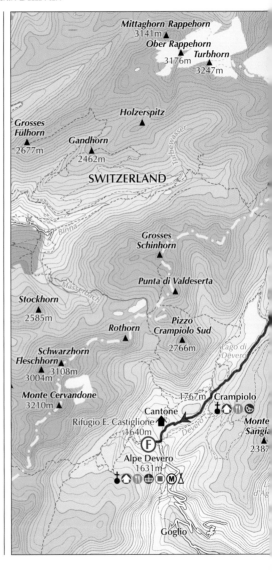

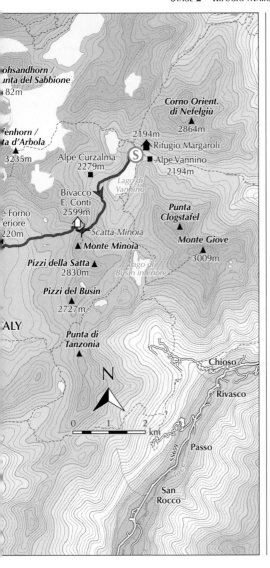

ohsandhorn /
nta del Sabbione
82m

**Corno Orient.
di Nefelgiù**
▲ 2864m

enhorn /
a d'Arbola
▲
3235m

Alpe Curzalma
2279m ■

2194m
▲ Rifugio Margaroli
Ⓢ ■ Alpe Vannino
2194m

*Lago di
Vannino*

Bivacco
E. Conti
2599m

**Punta
Clogstafel**
▲

e Forno
eriore
220m

Scatta Minoia

Monte Giove
▲
3009m

▲**Monte Minoia**

Pizzi della Satta ▲
2830m

*Lago di
Busin inferiore*

Pizzi del Busin
▲
2727m

ALY

**Punta di
Tanzonia**
▲

Chioso

N

Rivasco

0   1   2
▬▬▬▬▬▬▬ km

Passo

San
Rocco

45

the stream here. Continue ahead directly to the left of Alpe Forno Inferiore (2220m) and turn left along the broad track, across the stream by a bridge and follow the sign right downhill. Descend to a more level stretch, where it is easy to improve the pace. However, don't miss the small grassy path on your left that leaves the bigger track. If you do, no matter, the larger track will eventually lead you to the same place. As you start to descend through rock and trees, views of **Lago di Devero** appear ahead.

BAITA

Baita (pl. *baite*) is a term used in northern Italy to refer to small *alpe* huts typically of the central and western Alps. Constructed with dry-stone walls these are typically roofed with substantial stone slabs known as *piodi*, which provide protection from heavy winter snow. *Baite* are often clustered together in alpine pastures where they are occupied seasonally by herders tending sheep, cattle or goats during the summer. In recent years abandoned *baite* are being restored with varying degrees of respect, for holiday homes.

Re-join the vehicle track on a corner by a building marked as 'Spygher' (1901m). Continue on the track south-west for around 3km. On route a marked side track appears on the left. This shortcuts a drop in the main track but either will do. Shortly after the vehicle track loops right while the footpath continues straight ahead, again they re-join shortly after and descend on a steep rocky track into the settlement of **Crampiolo** (1767m).

Crampiolo is a good example of the trend for former *alpe* farming huts to be converted into holiday homes. Nonetheless, it is a beautiful spot that is clearly cared for with several outlets for traditional produce as well as an *albergo*, at least two restaurants, a water fountain and even public toilets!

Leave Crampiolo, past a restaurant and look for a track to the right, bounded by a rustic log fence. It is marked by a signpost to Alpe Devero (45min). Follow

this track as it weaves between trees, downhill alongside the Torrente Devero until you cross the bridge to reach **Alpe Devero** (1631m). Keep ahead until you cross a further bridge to reach the church and museum where you turn right. Here a GTA sign on your right is marked to H99 Alpe Veglia (6hr 15min). This is your direction out of Devero for the next stage.

The picturesque Crampiolo

> If you plan to overnight at **Rifugio E. Castiglione** just a little outside Alpe Devero to the north, it is worth taking the marked nature trail south-west from Crampiolo to Cantone (1640m) and the Rifugio Castiglione. It is then a short 0.5km walk south on the paved road and across the bridge, into the centre of Alpe Devero.

FACILITIES INFORMATION FOR STAGE 2

Accommodation

Bivvaco Ettore Conti, dormitory, Colle Scatta Minoia, 28863 Formazza, (VB), +39 0324 240449

Agriturismo Alpe Crampiolo, mixed rooms, wifi, Frazione Crampiolo, 13, Alpe Devero, 28861 Crampiolo (VB), +39 347 817 9494

Albergo Ristorante La Baita, double and triple rooms, wifi, Frazione Crampiolo, 28861 Crampiolo, (VB), +39 0324 619190

Rifugio Enrico Castiglione, mixed rooms, wifi, Località Cantone, 28861 Baceno, (VB), +39 0324 619126

Rifugio Sesto Calende, mixed rooms, wifi, Borgo Alpe Devero, 28845 Baceno, (VB), +39 0324 619149

Albergo La Lanca, double and family rooms, wifi, Borgo Alpe Devero, 74, 28861 Baceno, (VB), +39 0324 619135

Locanda Antico Alpino, mixed rooms, wifi, Via Alpe Devero, 53, 28861 Baceno (VB), +39 0324 619113

B&B Alpe Devero, double and family rooms, wifi, Località Balmavalle, 13, 28861 Alpe Devero, VB, +39 392 062 4036

Amenities

Local produce shop and a couple of restaurant/trattoria options at Crampiolo.

A wider choice of restaurants at Alpe Devero.

Transport

Prontobus run a service once a day in summer (at 18:23 in 2022) from the upper parking at Alpe Devero to Baceno where a further bus can take you out to Domodossola for onward train connections.

STAGE 3
Alpe Devero to Alpe Veglia

Start	Alpe Devero (1631m)
Finish	Alpe Veglia (1750m)
Distance	13km
Ascent	955m
Descent	835m
Time	5hr 30min

A wonderful stage with a climb through pine trees to the upper valley of the Rio Buscagna. This is a long gentle stretch among jagged peaks alongside the quiet waters of the *torrente*, which gurgle and flow between rocks, then coalesce in deep tranquil pools that invite a dip. It is tempting to linger here, but not too long. The latter stretch into Alpe Veglia demands a little more concentration and stamina, and in wet weather a potential minor detour if the slope below Pizzo Morro looks treacherous.

From the centre of **Alpe Devero** head west, past Albergo La Lanca then cross the bridge on your right, opposite Restaurante Alpino. Follow the road here to the end where you meet the cluster of old huts known as **Piedemonte** (1644m). Here red/white trail blazes guide you between houses and beyond to follow a path that now climbs directly up the slope north-west, with the *torrente* crashing over rocks below and to your left. Continue to climb what seems like a natural staircase

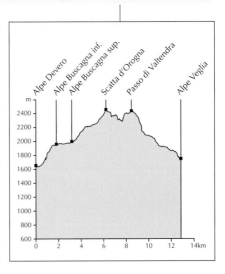

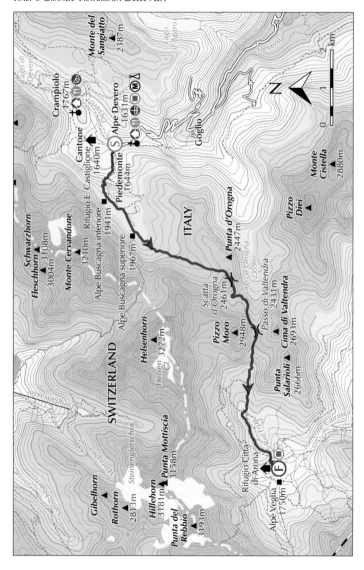

to emerge from the trees at the **Alpe Buscagna inferiore** (1941m). Continue ahead with sporadic trail blazes to mark your way, keeping the Rio di Buscagna on your left for about 1.3km to pass through the huts of **Alpe Buscagna superiore** (1967m) where a sign is marked to Alpe Veglia.

Climb gradually across the head of the valley, a rocky and barren landscape, to reach the high point of the day at **Scatta d'Orogna** (2461m). The signpost atop the *colle* indicates that Alpe Veglia is now 2hr 45min away. This is not so much of a pass or a *colle* as creeping around the shallow end of a great rock ridge that leads north-west up to the summit of Punta delle Caldaie (2853m). Meanwhile on your left, you walk parallel to the Valle Bondolero, a drop of several hundred metres below. Descend the narrow path south-west with care and around the north end of the seasonal **Lago d'Orogna** (2359m).

Bearing to the right, continue below the foreboding crags of Pizzo Moro (2948m). Care must be taken here, and a particularly exposed section is protected by chains. Do not linger if snow remains on the slopes above, it is prone to land slip and on a wet day wisdom might dictate a descent to the valley floor to climb from

The inviting Rio di Buscagna

the safer lower slopes. Climb across the steep hillside to reach the **Passo di Valtendra** (2431m) from where the going becomes easier.

After a short distance however, the west face of Pizzo Moro seems to descend impossibly steeply into the Pian del Scric. With some sharp switchbacks and considerable boulder hopping find your way down the small path at its side, after which the path levels to a more leisurely stroll along the upper basin of this valley. When you reach a rustic wooden water fountain at 2051m the path spilts. Keep right here, to descend through larch forest to a further water fountain. Here cross the *torrente* and pass directly in front of the *alpe* buildings, guided by a red/white blaze on the building corner. Beyond the building you will see a signpost, take the path across a 'two-log' bridge, and follow left across to and along the far side of the meadow following the Rio Frua until the path turns across another log bridge, then away from the stream and on through a long section of shrub and trees, eventually into Cornu (1750m), one of several small hamlets that make up **Alpe Veglia** (1750m).

FACILITIES INFORMATION FOR STAGE 3

Accommodation

Rifugio Citta di Arona, mixed rooms, 28865 Alpe Veglia, (VB), +39 339 404 6395

Albergo Lepontino, double and family rooms, 28868 Alpe Veglia, (VB), +39 375 500 9414

Albergo Alpino Monte Leone, double and family rooms, 28868 Alpe Veglia, (VB), +39 388 769 8751

Amenities

Meals and limited bar snacks available at rifugio and albergos.

Mini-market at Albergo Alpino Monte Leone.

Transport

Prontobus run a service four times a day from Ponte Campo (at the foot of the mullatiera below Alpe Veglia) to Varzo, from where a Comazzibus connection can be taken to Domodossola and onward trains.

STAGE 4
Alpe Veglia to Varzo

Start	Alpe Veglia (1750m)
Finish	Varzo (568m)
Distance	18.75km
Ascent	820m
Descent	2035m
Time	7hr 45 min

An early option on the stage between an adventurous path across steep ground, or the lower track should be influenced by the weather. The high path is only for dry days. The climb beyond is on good paths leading to an epic valley view. The descent to Varzo is steep initially, softening in the lower slopes with a long level stretch to visit a scenic gorge. From Trasquera the route takes in one of the best preserved ancient *mulattiera* you are likely to see.

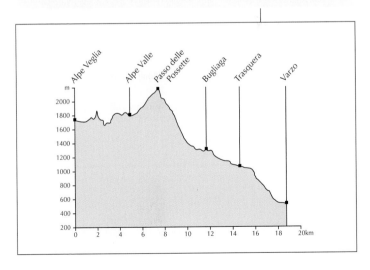

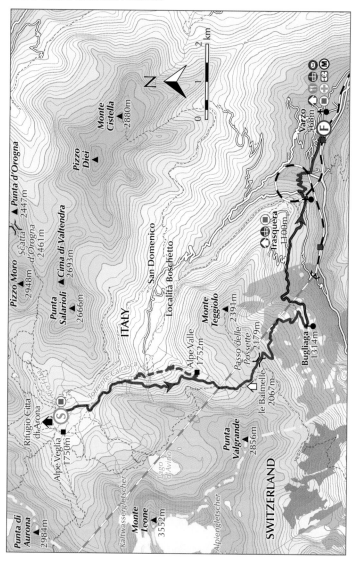

From **Alpe Veglia** follow the main vehicle track south-east along the valley keeping the *torrente* initially on your right and passing a couple of tributaries. Cross over a wooden bridge, and soon after another. Keep left at the signed junction then continue on this broad track as it winds its way along the side of the deep gorge, now on your left. After about 30min you pass a hut your left and the track begins to descend through switchbacks. ▸ A short way beyond the GTA rises from the track on the right on a tiny path across precipitous slopes. This is a fun adventure with a little scrambling, protected in exposed places. Scramble up the initial bank where a rope is provided, then a clearer, if narrow, path becomes apparent. Continue south below crags for an undulating traverse making use of rope or chains where provided to give security on this airy and adventurous section. If it is wet however, or you are particularly averse to slope exposure, this is not great option and a much easier alternate can be taken.

An easier alternate route can be taken from here.

Alternate route
Continue down the main vehicle track through four successive switchbacks. At a hut on the left the path turns away from the *torrente* and steeply downhill to cross a tributary stream, then around two more switchbacks. Shortly after, the path divides at a fork with a signpost. Take the track going right uphill past a couple of summer residences and through more switchbacks, until you reach the meadow slope of **Alpe Valle** at a comprehensive signpost. Here you re-join the main route.

Main route
Eventually the track becomes easier and reaches **Alpe Valle** (1752m) at a comprehensive signpost, where the alternate path re-joins the route. Continue to climb uphill on the track through Alpe Stalletto (1847m). Markings reveal paths that shortcut the track if not overgrown, but the track continues as far as **le Balmelle** (2067m) from where a path marked by a blaze on a rock climbs left to the **Passo delle Possette** (2179m). Crossing the unusual

The high path to Alpe Valle is great on dry days

lip of rock continue to the brow of the hill where the valley is laid out before you.

The path is clear for a way now as it switchbacks down the hillside. The first time it becomes unclear is a long traverse left across the hillside. Just keep going across the long grass until you pick up red/white blazes on an old *baita*. Pass to the left of this and the path becomes clearer. As you finally emerge onto a gravel track at Casa Grande (1412m) follow it around to the right signed *Trasquera*. Reach a junction and turn left downhill.

At **Bugliaga** (1314m) you meet the road. Turn left again and enjoy the more level road for a while. Continue on for some time, via an incredible gorge that takes you through a tunnel and over an impossibly high arched bridge at the Ponte del Diavolo (1228m), eventually down through the hamlets of **Trasquera** to a beautiful church on the brow of the hill. Follow the sign here that guides you down through trees onto a fantastic old *mulattiera* that is your track for much of the remaining descent.

When you finally reach the bottom of these cobbles, take a moment to reflect on how many there were and that fact that every one was laid by hand, before passing under the railway ahead by a small arch and down to the road junction. A signpost on your right here points across the road and ahead to Passo Variola (2252m) marked GTA. For now if it is your choice, turn left and follow the road into **Varzo**.

FACILITIES INFORMATION FOR STAGE 4

Accommodation

Agriturismo La Fraccia, double rooms, 28868 Trasquera, (VB), +39 0324 79120

B&B Alpe Veglia, double and twin rooms, Via Colle 57, Varzo, (VB), +39 0324 72244, +39 333 406 6271

Hotel Sempione, double and family rooms, Viale Castelli, 70, 28868 Varzo (VB), +39 335 565 2523

B&B I Lamponi, double rooms, Via Cattagna, 17, 28868 Varzo (VB), +39 347 565 0886

Amenities

Meals and limited bar snacks available at Agriturismo La Fraccia and Hotel Sempione.

Small shop (*alimentari*) in Trasquera.

Several restaurant options, ATM, pharmacy and post office in Varzo.

Transport

Prontobus run a service four times a day from Trasquera to Varzo, from where a Comazzibus connection can be taken to Domodossola and onward trains.

STAGE 5

Varzo to Rifugio San Bernardo

Start	Varzo (568m)
Finish	Rifugio San Bernardo (1628m)
Distance	16km
Ascent	1755m
Descent	655m
Time	7hr

The climb out of Varzo is a steep one that twists back and forth up a largely dry hillside, so carry sufficient water. In the autumn, locals gather mushrooms here, they are prolific on the heavily wooded hillside. Higher up feels wilder, and there is plenty of evidence of wild boar. Crossing the pass, the going becomes easier and water plentiful. A sun-baked Alpe Dorca seems abandoned but marks the beginning of the descent towards the forest, shade and rest.

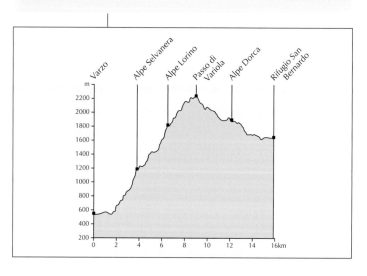

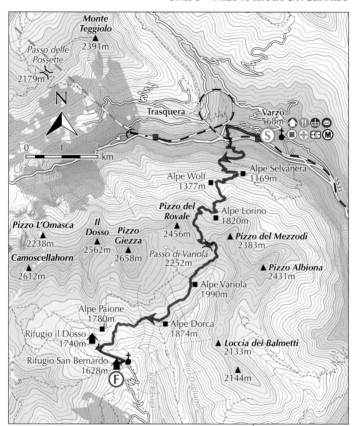

From Varzo, return to the main road and head north-west back to the road junction at the base of the descent in the previous stage. At the road junction turn left (or straight across if you have not been into Varzo) and descend to a corner where the road bears left. Instead, turn right between the houses and follow a narrow path down a slope. It can be overgrown here. Descend to a low arch under the road and railway, pass under and beyond past bee hives, turn right out to a hydro-electric plant service road, then left across a bridge that appears to lead only to a dark tunnel. Turn right immediately before the tunnel entrance then left at a signpost for Passo Variola and take the path uphill into the trees.

Cross a service road several times and continue steeply uphill before the track becomes the remnants of a once good *mulattiera*. Beyond this the path becomes a fairly arduous set of steep switches up the hillside, however on the plus side there is light tree cover and often a light breeze here. As the path finally begins to level take a glance down the steep side into Varzo before bearing right into the clearing of **Alpe Selvanera** (1169m). Pass directly between the buildings, then turn right across in front of them to find the track ahead. There is a water tap on the front of the main hut, this and a spring a little further on are normally the only water until after the pass, so take what you need.

Continue to wind your way uphill although marginally less steep now until you reach **Alpe Wolf** (1377m). Cross the meadow to the left of the huts and into the trees beyond. The path from here is steep and with much dense shrub so can be hard going until you reach **Alpe Lorino** (1820m). Note the *bivacco* here is private, not open to public use, and there is no water. A wooden bench in the shade of an ash tree is heaven after that climb, however!

Keeping the huts on your right, continue following sporadic blazes that twist and wind their way ever upwards to crest a ridge line where the open breeze is welcome, but one more dip and climb remain before the *colle*. As you rise for the final ascent it is easy to lose the way markings on the ground. The path cuts to the right of the 'face' ahead then sharply left to cross above it. It is easy to miss this, but a glance back from higher ground reveals markings. Once above this keep left, don't head for the high point, you actually descend slightly from where you have climbed, to the **Passo di Variola** (2252m).

About 10min after the pass you meet the first stream, fed by a spring just up the slope, and it is so welcome! When you have passed your 6th or 7th stream, or lost

count altogether, you start to wonder why just a little of this water couldn't flow down the other side of the hill!

Follow the path as it meanders along the hillside now, following the rock blazes to the intriguing **Alpe Dorca**, a crazy run-down place sweltering in the heat on the hillside that is more than a little reminiscent of a scene from a western movie.

Continue along the trail, eventually descending to Casariola (1727m) to a trail junction and sign guiding you right, towards the torrent and the huts beyond. Cross the *torrente*, then left along the hillside, between abandoned huts, continuing for quite a way before rising a little to a track junction and signpost straight on for San Bernardo. Descend to the road and follow it over the river and round to the left, continuing until you reach a three-way track junction. Take the middle path and **Rifugio San Bernardo** (1628m) is ahead on your right.

Alpe Dorca is evocative of the wild west

FACILITIES INFORMATION FOR STAGE 5

Accommodation

Rifugio il Dosso, mixed rooms, wifi, Alpe Arza, 28842 Bognanco (VB), +39 366 263 0583

Rifugio San Bernardo, mixed rooms, wifi, Alpe San Bernardo, 28842, Bognanco (VB), +39 338 788 4574

Amenities

Meals and limited bar snacks available at *rifugios*.

Transport

None on route.

STAGE 6

Rifugio San Bernardo to Alpe Cheggio

Start	Rifugio San Bernardo (1628m)
Finish	Alpe Cheggio (1497m)
Distance	16km
Ascent	1055m
Descent	1200m
Time	6hr 45min

A fabulous stage though scenic country that enables the distance to be covered easily. Long sections of traverse at a gentle gradient, albeit at times on a narrow and occasionally eroded track, lead to stunning views above the turquoise Lago Alpe dei Cavalli.

Turn left out of the **Rifugio San Bernardo**, back to the track junction, turn right, then immediately right again after the church following the signpost to Passo della Preja. A short way on the track rises to the right to detour a property, otherwise the route is easy to follow and largely contours the mountainside. Keep ahead as the track narrows,

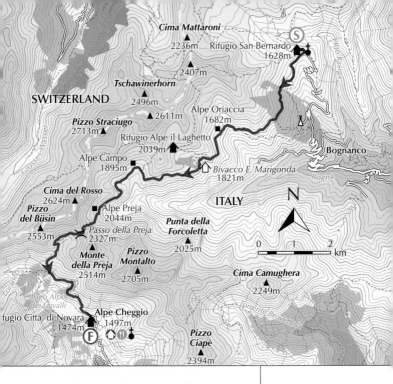

passing a track junction for Pizzanco where a sign suggests it is 3hr 55min to Passo della Preja. Look back over your left shoulder as you climb to the Croce del Vallaro for excellent views across Domodossola. Crest the rise and enjoy a small descent across the meadow to **Bivacco E. Marigonda** (1821m) which can provide water and a comfortable rest stop or overnight stay if you are self-sufficient.

Continue up to the right side of the hut and around the back to the left to a signpost noting around 3hr to the pass, and begin the next climb following a narrow path across grassy slopes. After a long undulating traverse a little ascent must be relinquished for the passage around the hillside to **Alpe Campo** (1895m). This hut would make a reasonable bivouac stop with good floor, above the cattle shed, with steps up and an unlocked door.

Crystal clear water at Alpe Campo

The path can be a little hard to spot here in undergrowth, but continues across in front of the huts. This challenge continues as far as **Alpe Preja** and requires careful spotting of faded blazes on rocks. Alpe Preja (2044m) is effectively a cave formed under a boulder adapted as a shelter. It seems neither the map nor the signpost guide you correctly here. The sign suggests you continue past the *alpe* for a way before climbing right. This is difficult and does not follow the marked track on the ground or accompanying blazes. Climb directly up behind the *alpe* to find the path ascending to a prominent rise, the path is much clearer from here on.

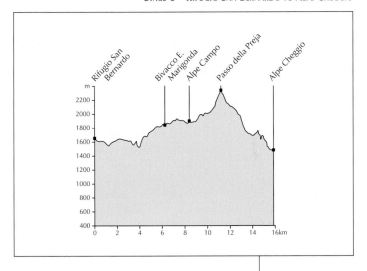

Cross the Passo della Preja (2327m) and descend ahead keeping to the right over a small rise. Continue contouring the right side of the valley to reach a signpost at some hut remains, where a hard left will see you descend behind a hump towards the *torrente*. Descending to the stream, you follow this down through a narrow gorge. Don't miss a big rock in the middle of the river where you want to cross. The trail blaze is on the downstream side so it is easy to miss. The path is much better on the other side and gradually bears left through shrub and light tree cover. As you descend the path continues around to the left where footing requires care as this hillside can become quite overgrown. Reaching a signpost beside the rubble of some old huts, keep left across a meadow then continue parallel to the lakeside below.

From what still seems like a long way above **Alpe Cheggio**, begin the descent of the switchbacks that deliver you to the base of the dam and road, turn left and follow the road up, between houses, where the Albergo Alpino is on your left. If you are heading to the *rifugio*, then directly opposite the *albergo* is a small church and

Low water behind the dam at Cheggio

notice board, to the left of that you will find a red/white blaze on a post that marks a path descending between houses to the *rifugio*.

FACILITIES INFORMATION FOR STAGE 6

Accommodation

Rifugio Citta di Novara, mixed rooms, Via Guida Alpina Marani, 1, 28841 Antrona Schieranco, (VB), +39 0324 571256

Albergo Ristorante Alpino, double and family rooms, Cheggio, 28841 Antronapiana, Antrona Schieranco, (VB), +39 0324 575975

Amenities

Meals and limited bar snacks available at *rifugio* and *albergos*.

Transport

None on route.

STAGE 7
Alpe Cheggio to Molini

Start	Alpe Cheggio (1497m)
Finish	Molini (485m)
Distance	18.75km
Ascent	985m
Descent	1985m
Time	7hr 15min

A longer stage with the option to break at the atmospheric Rifugio Alpe della Colma, high on the ridge above Molini. A long and gradual descent starts the stage, with refreshments possible in Antronapiana and San Pietro, before the steep climb under trees to the Alpe della Colma. The descent to Molini is a fascinating journey back in time, if sometimes hard on the knees!

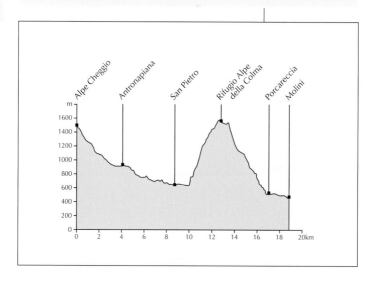

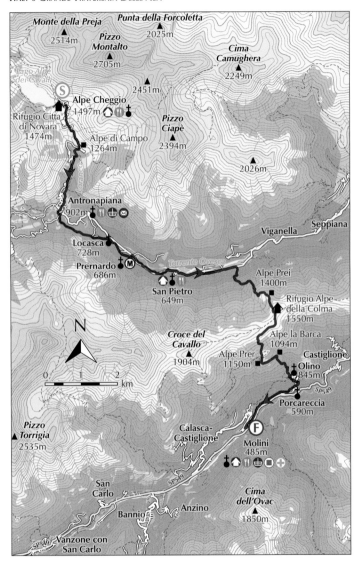

Monte della Preja
2514m

Punta della Forcoletta
2025m

Pizzo
Montalto
2705m

Cima
Camughera
2249m

2451m

S Alpe Cheggio
1497m

Rifugio Città
di Novara
1474m

Alpe di Campo
1264m

Pizzo
Ciapè
2394m

2026m

Antronapiana
902m

Viganella

Seppiana

Locasca
728m

Torrente Ovesca

Prernardo
686m

Alpe Prei
1400m

San Pietro
649m

Rifugio Alpe
della Colma
1550m

Alpe la Barca
1094m

N

Croce del
Cavallo
1904m

Alpe Prer
1150m

Castiglione
Olino
845m

0   1   2
km

SP549

Pizzo
Torrigia
2535m

Porcareccia
590m

Calasca-
Castiglione

F Molini
485m

San
Carlo

SP549

Anzino

Cima
dell'Ovac
1850m

Bannio

SP549

Vanzone con
San Carlo

If you are leaving **Alpe Cheggio** from the *albergo*, initially take the path beside the church opposite, that leads down between houses, following the blazes to the *rifugio* and road. From the *rifugio* take the road south initially. Trail blazes marked on rocks and trees guide the way across numerous switchbacks of the road, shortening the overall descent. Shortly after **Alpe di Campo** the path remains with the road to Alpe Pianzei, then the track, more clearly an old *mulattiera* at this stage, leads into **Antronapiana** (902m).

Following the blazes through the backstreets of Antronapiana can be an adventure leading to unexpected discoveries. Whichever way you come through the town, find your way to the main road and river at the bottom of the hill and cross either one of the two crossings over the river to converge on the road corner by a series of shrines. Take the left fork of the road and pass the cemetery to the road end then follow the broad gravel track ahead. Ignore a side track to Rovesca and keep past a helpfully placed water fountain, on downhill under trees, then right under a bridge and follow the *mulattiera* downhill. Touching the road momentarily, take the right and continue to a further section of road into **Locasca**.

At Locasca take the right at a fork in the track, along a tiny lane between old houses, then continue until you descend to the church and past a playground and across pasture. The track descends to the main road, turn right and follow this for a short way until markings guide you off road again. This continues for some way, alternating between the road and small sections of track running broadly parallel with the road. Continue through the hamlets of **San Pietro** and Prato then, shortly after a sports ground on the left, turn right onto a track, beside an information board and signpost, leading steeply uphill into the woods. Pass the hut at Alpe Baitone and continue steeply uphill eventually through a clearing where **Alpe Prei** sits, then after a further wooded stretch reach **Rifugio Alpe della Colma** (1550m).

This is an atmospheric spot to overnight, but if you are continuing to Molini, head over the ridge and bear right along a long, level terrace past the remains of old

*Shrines are a
common sight
alongside the trail*

huts. After a way turn left steeply downhill, to the huts
and shrine at **Alpe Prer** (1150m). Here turn left again
and follow the terrace along the hill to summer homes
at **Alpe la Barca** (1094m). Now turn right and descend
more steeply once more, following regular markings, to
reach the shrine at the road's end. Continue down a track
to **Olino** (845m), past a church then right to a shrine at
the road corner. Here a track heads south-west through
the woods to Vigino just above Molini. This is the quicker
route, but for the more interesting original, turn left along
the road and take the right steeply downhill through trees,
shortcutting road bends and then below Crotto, following it for a short way behind a church. This fabulous old

mulattiera is like a step back in time, following narrow cobbled alleys between old stone dwellings, under arches where there is little to suggest we live in the era of the internet and mobile phones! Continue to the more modern houses in **Molini** (485m) and drop to the main road.

FACILITIES INFORMATION FOR STAGE 7

Accommodation

Rifugio Alpe della Colma, mixed rooms, Alpe Colma, 28873 Calasca-castiglione (VB), +39347 902 0098

Locanda del Tiglio, double and family rooms, wifi, Frazione Gurva, 7B, 28873 Molini, Calasca-castiglione (VB), +39 0324 81122

Azienda Agricola Madalu, mixed rooms, wifi, Frazione Molini, 10, 28873 Molini, (VB), +39 347 168 6357

Amenities

Meals and limited bar snacks available at Rifugio Alpe della Colma and accommodation providers in Molini.

Shops, restaurants and Post Office at Antronapiana.

Restaurant at San Pietro.

Restaurant at Molini.

Transport

Comazzibus run a service from Antrona Piana to Domodossola, also stopping at San Pietro, four times a day (weekdays).

Comazzibus also run a service from Molini to Domodossola six times a day on weekdays, twice at the weekend.

STAGE 8

Molini to Campello Monti

Start	Molini (485m)
Finish	Campello Monti (1305m)
Distance	15.75km
Ascent	1820m
Descent	990m
Time	7hr 15min

A varied stage commencing among trees along the *torrente*, a long climb in the shade is rewarded with brilliant views as far as the Valais ranges of Switzerland. Trail marking is adequate, a couple of eroded sections require care, but the path is rarely difficult to follow. Two unmanned huts along the route offer either shelter, or the opportunity to break the stage into smaller chunks.

If you are using the IGC Map 10, be aware that it inaccurately depicts the position of the trail in relation to the road on the initial departure from Molini.

◀ From the Locanda del Tiglio, on the main road through **Molini** (a hamlet in the parish of Calasca-Castiglione)

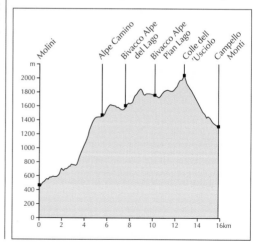

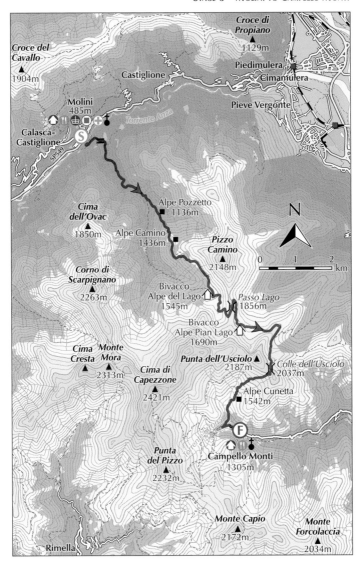

turn left, south-west, walking downhill for 1min. Just past a triple garage, the GTA leaves the road to the left, south, clearly marked with a Via-Alpina trail board, down a short flight of steps and across grass, leading to an ancient bridge across the gorge of the Torrente Anza and under the arches of the church of the Madonna della Gurva.

> The pilgrimage church of the **Madonna della Gurva** was built after a number of unexplained events occurred within a short space of time, including the oozing of blood from the image of the Virgin at a small primitive chapel that was then considered to be sacred. The location is spectacular, directly on the river, both resting on and balanced by a huge boulder. On 15th August of every year, the Feast Dedicated to Our Lady of the Assumption is celebrated here, with the presence of the traditional Militia of Calasca.

Crossing the gorge at Madonna della Gurva

On the far side of the bridge, turn initially left, north-east, and then immediately right following well-marked

switchbacks south climbing through thick shrubs and trees to a small road. Turn left here and follow the road until it crosses a stone bridge over the river and then keep right on the old *mulattiera* as it bears south-east and gradually ascends the Val Segnara. As the track narrows to a path, a helpful signpost confirms the direction. Several tributaries are crossed as you keep the main *torrente* to your right. At a further bridge keep left at the track junction. The path now leaves the valley and climbs steeply, still south-east, under the shade of chestnut trees that let little light through to the woodland floor, all the way up the ridgeline, past **Alpe Pozzetto** (1136m), with little more than occasional views afforded east into Valle Rosin, until you emerge into sunlight (on a good day) at **Alpe Camino** (1436m). The walking now becomes easier as the path contours to the right around the south of the ridge, variously through open and wooded sections. A couple of eroded sections need care, before the view opens up and you reach a short, exposed descent that is partially protected by cables. The unmanned hut **Bivacco Alpe del Lago** (1545m) rests in the base of the cirque ahead across a small bridge. ▶

Leaving Alpe del Lago re-cross the small bridge and head east across the, at times overgrown, path to climb around the back of the large rock to your right. As the path ascends below the Colle Camino and turns south, a dramatic gorge carved through the rock is revealed on the right. The path climbs steadily back and forth through springy alpenrose shrub, prone to becoming overgrown by mid-summer, before turning unexpectedly north-east to ascend the ridge. The path here is a little eroded and littered with trailing roots so care is required as you climb to Passo Lago (1856m) from where views extend to Monte Rosa and the Swiss peaks beyond on a clear day. Leaving the pass continue north-east, downhill, until the path turns decisively south to traverse the slope keeping fairly level until you reach **Bivacco Alpe Pian Lago** (1690m). The path continues a traverse broadly east ascending below a prominent ridge (1881m) on your right, before turning sharply right to cross over the

Note that Bivacco Alpe del Lago is referred to as Bivacco A. Pirozzini on the IGC map. Previously described as grotty, this hut now appears well cared for and equipped.

ridge via an unnamed *colle* (1831m), then right again to a slight descent south below the **Punta dell'Usciolo** (2187m), crossing the outflow of Lago di Ravinella before climbing once more to **Colle dell'Usciolo** (2037m). The descent south-west that follows is gradual and well-marked. Passing between buildings at **Alpe Cunetta** (1542m) then crossing first a tributary, and then the main stream, your destination comes into view as you pass the shrine at Alpe Orlo. The path passes above the small town to join a bigger track climbing south-west, however a left turn, north-east here will take you downhill into Campello Monti (1305m). Several small paths diverge as you approach **Campello Monti**, keep ahead to the church then descend cobbled stone steps, past the *posto tappa* in the old school building on your left, past local information boards. Look for the bridge across a tributary to the comfortable locanda and restaurant for food, rooms or keys to the *posto tappa*.

FACILITIES INFORMATION FOR STAGE 8

Accommodation

Bivacco Alpe del Lago, dormitory, unmanned

Bivacco Alpe Pian Lago, dormitory, unmanned

Locanda Alla Vetta del Capezzone, double and family rooms, wifi, Via Zamponi, 5, 28897 Valstrona, (VB), +39 0323 885113

Albergo Nigritella, double rooms, wifi, Via P. Zamponi, 4, 28897 Valstrona, (VB), +39 339 2988893

Amenities

Meals and limited bar snacks available at accommodation providers.

Transport

None on route.

STAGE 9

Campello Monti to Rifugio Alpe Baranca

Start	Campello Monti (1305m)
Finish	Rifugio Alpe Baranca (1600m)
Distance	18.75km
Ascent	1635m
Descent	1345m
Time	8hr 30min

A varied and interesting stage. Alpine meadows and summer farms lead to the first pass and a well-made path takes you swiftly down again to Rimella where refreshments and supplies are available. The gentle climb to a second *colle* offers great views, a water fountain and nearby refreshments. The descent meanders back and forth between clusters of traditional homes and meadows to the friendly *rifugio* at Alpe Baranca.

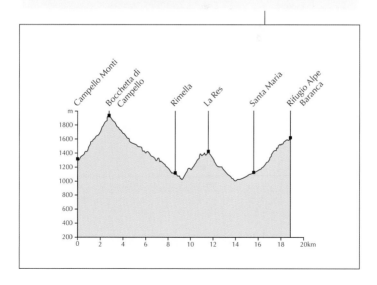

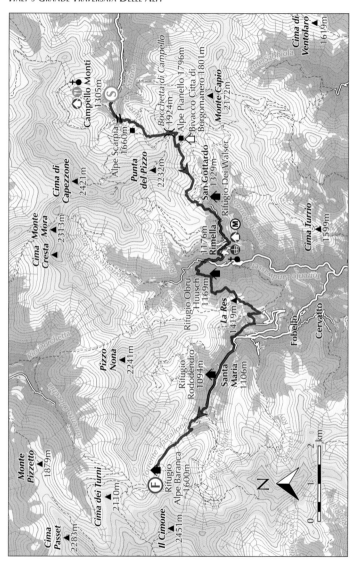

Take the track south-west out of **Campello Monti**. After 10min cross a small bridge and follow the path through switchbacks left up the valley. After a signpost the path becomes a bit indistinct below Alpe del Vecchio. Keep right ascending to the craggy outcrop above and the path becomes clear again. Continue up the valley south-west, pass **Alpe Scarpia** shortly before bearing left to cross the *torrente* on rocks at the head of the valley, and commence the steeper section of the climb to the **Bocchetta di Campello** (1924m) marked with a cross. Descend south, then turn sharply right and contour around the slope before dropping to a lower path out of **Alpe Pianello** (1796m). Cross several streams then enter woodland just below Alpe Selletta, where a path to the left leads to **Rifugio dei Walser** 10min away in **San Gottardo**. Continue into the trees soon passing the curious chapel and rock overhang at Posa dei Morti.

> Until 1551 **Campello Monti** had neither church nor cemetery. The deceased would be carried over the same path you travel, to their resting place in Rimella. The pallbearers would rest at Posa dei Morti (literally 'the laying of the dead') before the priest from Rimella could perform the final rites. Due to the difficulty of the pass crossing in winter those deceased late in the year would be stored in a frozen condition before making their final journey in the spring.

Just beyond the Posa dei Morti keep right at a track junction marked for Rimella, and after 10min keep left at the next small junction, heading downhill to meet the road. Turn right and follow the road for 5min then take the well-marked path left through the hamlets of **Rimella**; first Sella then Prati where you emerge alongside a well-kept former hotel (selling refreshments). Beyond, the path is marked left of the church, downhill along cobbled streets to Chiesa (1176m) and Albergo Fontana (*posto tappa*, restaurant and *alimenteri*).

To continue drop down to the road and turn right. Continue to the corner and take the path signposted right, across the Torrente Landwasser and uphill through Roncaccio Inferiore (1124m), then on up to Roncaccio Superiore (1205m).

RONCACCIO INFERIORE

The 'ghost' hamlet of Roncaccio Inferiore consists of a few buildings in a precarious state of preservation. Two examples of old Walser homes are met, the first on the right of the track has a carpentry room and in the living quarters an old stone hearth is still present. A little further on another example with original roof frame of wooden beams has the remains of a fresco on the wall opposite the track. Up a couple of stone ramps, the church is dedicated to the Blessed Virgin of the Graces and dates back to 1705 when it was built, according to historical documents, for 625 Imperial Lire. A little further on some of the dwellings of Roncaccio Superiore are under renovation. The older of the two hamlets, dating from as early as 1484, it is built around a small square with a panoramic view. Facing onto the square, the old washhouse, with wash tubs of monolithic stone, was the main meeting point for the Walser community here. The church, built in the early 18th century, is dedicated to the visitation of Mary to Saint Elizabeth. The square is accessed by passing under a 'barrel vault arch' of dry stone below an old building on the left of the track just before it proceeds up old stone steps between buildings. The building under which the arch passes was originally constructed around 1650, then later renovated in 2005 to become the simple, but characterful Rifugio Obru Huusch (1169m). With just 3 rooms, plus a kitchen, dining and communal area on the 1st floor, strategically placed for the GTA.

Continue uphill, cross a stream then bear south-west. Emerging from trees climb to the *colle* at **La Res** (1419m). Be aware the water fountain here is frequented by animals. An information board provides contacts for several accommodation options around Fobello.

Fans of the automobile would be encouraged to make the descent into **Fobello**, perhaps warranting an overnight stay, as the small town was the birthplace of Vincenzo Lancia (1881–1937) the

The water fountain
at La Res

famous car designer and racing driver. The town now houses a permanent museum celebrating the achievements of its most famous resident.

Leaving the *colle*, descend south-west to Belvedere, then take an abrupt right just before the buildings to descend towards the chapel at San Antonio. As you enter the trees turn left again to descend past a house and out onto the track leading into Boco superiore (1089m). Turn right and follow the marked track through houses, then on to la Piana (1027m). Descend to the road, turn right and follow the road alongside the Torrente Mastallone through **Santa Maria** (1106m), where the rustic *posto tappa* is on the right before the chapel, where the road ends at la Gazza. Continue on the track, past the last house then turn immediately right on the well-marked path, which resumes a north-west direction after crossing a stream. Climb steeply at first, then cross to the west bank of the *torrente*, continuing past the initial huts of Alpe Baranca (1566m) on the right, before the more obvious **Rifugio Alpe Baranca** (1600m) comes into view.

81

The unique Rifugio Alpe Baranca

FACILITIES INFORMATION FOR STAGE 9

Accommodation

Rifugio dei Walser, double and twin rooms, Frazione S, 13020 San Gottardo, (VC), +39 338 976 1975

Albergo Walser House, double and twin rooms, Via per San Gottardo, 13020 Sella (VC) +39 347 366 3960

Albergo Fontana, double and twin rooms, Localita' Centro 15, 13020 Rimella (VC), +39 0163 55200

Rifugio Obru Huusch, double and twin rooms, SP80, 13020 Rimella, (VC), +39 393 756 9591

Posto Tappa GTA, Santa Maria di Fobello, Frazione Santa Maria di Fobello, (VC), +39 0163 55008

Rifugio Alpe Baranca, dormitory, la Gazza di, Localita' Alpe Baranca, 13025 Frazione Campo, (VC), +39 347 865 9385

Amenities

Meals and limited bar snacks available at accommodation providers.

Small shop selling staples located within Albergo Fontana in Rimella.

Transport

None on route.

STAGE 10
Rifugio Alpe Baranca to Carcoforo

Start	Rifugio Alpe Baranca (1600m)
Finish	Carcoforo (1304m)
Distance	8.5km
Ascent	655m
Descent	950m
Time	4hr

A shorter stage that is worth taking your time over. An initial short climb alongside the cascading *torrente* warrants frequent pauses to take in the views. The initial crest opens up the picturesque Lago Baranca lying in a cirque of surrounding ridges, and the interesting and historic settlement of Alpe Selle. Beyond, a scenic and gradual ascent to Colle d'Egua provides a stunning viewpoint west to Monte Rosa. An equally gradual descent is no less rewarding, while an early finish and a stay at the welcoming Albergo Alpenrose is a treat in every way.

Leaving **Rifugio Alpe Baranca**, return to the main path and turn right. As the path steepens a single switchback draws you away from the *torrente* before turning back towards the outflow of **Lago di Baranca** at the head of this initial climb. Pass along the east end of the lake where (on a good day) the mirror-still morning water offers reflections of the surrounding ridges. A small effort brings you to **Alpe Selle** (1824m) and a tempting water fountain just below the Colle Baranca and the old chapel. Follow the *mulattiera* north-west, passing among the fascinating old buildings, which suggest a

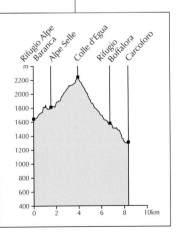

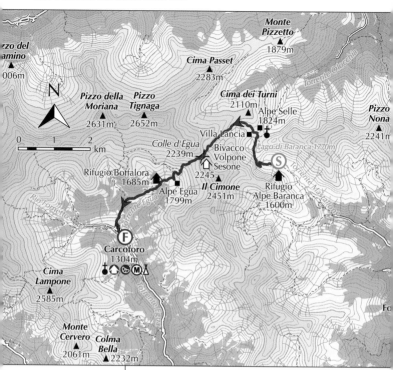

more prosperous time. A faded inscription still marks the remains of a modest hotel here and, while an intervening period of decline has passed, some of the former summer homes have now undergone restoration. At the end of the buildings turn right and climb around the southern flank of Cima dei Turni (2110m).

Beyond Alpe Selle, an elegant and dramatic ruin is perched dramatically on a commanding outcrop, the former summer retreat of racing driver Vincenzo Lancia (1881–1937) was once a magnificent villa. Designed in 1908 by Costantino Gilodi, a Borgosean architect, the villa was bought by the

Lancia family, who renamed it **'Aprilia'**, after the famous model of the car manufacturer. After the armistice of 8 September 1943, the path became an escape route to Switzerland and the villa was used by the partisans. In April 1944 the villa suffered a fire during a battle between partisans and fascists. Since then, the villa has been abandoned and today is in a severe state of decay, in ruins and unsafe, although it is still owned by the Lancia family.

A gradual ascent brings you to the **Colle d'Egua** (2239m). A short way up the ridge on the left is the **Bivacco Volpone Sesone** (2245m). Descend southwest through switchbacks, passing huts at Alpe Sellette (1915m) and **Alpe Egua** (1799m). Cross a stream to a fork in the path. Keep right to visit **Rifugio Boffalora** (1685m). Pass several huts then across a small bridge affording a scenic photo of the waterfall on the Rio Passone. A short descent through trees brings you to the outlying buildings of **Carcoforo**. Descend past the church to the main road and turn left downhill a short way where on your left is the Agriturismo Bruc. Albergo

The former home of racing car legend Vincenzo Lancia

Alpenrose is on the right. A little further down the road a campsite is also available.

Alongside the Albergo Alpenrose, and worth a visit, the **Alta Valsesia Park visitor's centre** occupies a restored traditional Walser house.

FACILITIES INFORMATION FOR STAGE 10

Accommodation

Rifugio Alpino Alpe Selle, mixed rooms, Baranca, 13025 Fobello, (VC), +39 347 262 2880

Bivacco Volpone Sesone, dormitory, Colle d'Egua

Rifugio Boffalora, dormitory, Sentiero, 122, 13026 Carcoforo, (VC), +39 339 607 6910

Agriturismo Alpe Bruc, mixed rooms, wifi, Localita' Alpe Bruc, 13026 Carcoforo, (VC), +39 0163 95600

La Case del Folletto B&B, double rooms, wifi, Via Centro, 34, 13026 Carcoforo, (VC), +39 348 145 9416

Rifugio Albergo Alpenrose, double and family rooms, wifi, Località Tetto Minocco, 12, 13026 Carcoforo, (VC), +39 0163 174 0608

Amenities

Meals and limited bar snacks available at accommodation providers except B&B.

A couple of good restaurant options including Albergo Alpenrose.

Basic farm produce shop in Carcoforo.

Transport

None on route.

STAGE 11

Carcoforo to Rima

Start	Carcoforo (1304m)
Finish	Rima (1411m)
Distance	9.5km
Ascent	1055m
Descent	925m
Time	4hr 45min

After a gentle warm-up, a steep climb and descent is the main feature of this stage. As you approach the head of the valley and peer up at the precipitous ridges above it seems hard to imagine how the track will ascend so steeply. Nonetheless, a manageable route up is gradually revealed and, taken steadily, is quite a rewarding approach with a refreshing mountain spring encountered on the way.

From **Carcoforo**, follow the road west up the valley, keeping the *torrente* on your left. Ignore the first bridge and keep ahead as the road becomes a gravel track. After around 1km the track takes a sharp left at the head of the valley across the Rio Fornetto. Follow the well-worn path up, keeping left at a fork, and between the huts at **Alpe Selva Bruna** (1464m) where the main work of the climb begins through lush vegetation. Ascend slowly, taking time to pause regularly and admire the view back east as the sun rises over Carcoforo. At Transinera Bella (1925m) a mountain spring emerges (just to the left of the huts). Continue up past the remains of

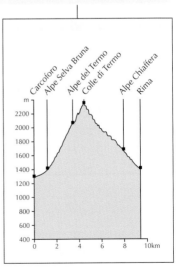

further huts at **Alpe del Termo**, where much of the vegetation is left behind and the terrain becomes the rock and scree of the upper mountain, then follow the switchbacks to reach **Colle del Termo** (2351m).

As you cross the *colle*, the path to your right offers the opportunity for a 10min side excursion to the high point of **Cima del Tiglio** (2545m), although this does little to add to the already tremendous views you have of the surrounding mountains.

To descend towards Rima, leave the *colle* on the path to your left which contours a short way before beginning

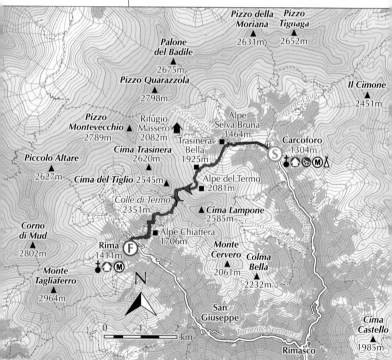

Descending into Rima

a seemingly relentless series of switchbacks down the steep slope. The path has been improved here over the years and although the slope is steep, the way is never difficult. You are around half way down when the path enters forest and the carpet of pine needles certainly softens the descent. **Alpe Chiaffera** (1706m) offers the opportunity of drinking water before the remaining section. As you round a final corner the beautifully laid-out terraces of **Rima** (1411m) come into view on your left with a waterfall cascading from the plateau beyond. Turn left into the lane and pass a church, continuing to the main square and water fountain, noting the GTA sign on the wall of a lane off to your right, your way onward when you are ready to continue.

FACILITIES INFORMATION FOR STAGE 11

Accommodation

Posto Tappa (Keys at restaurant Grillo Brillo/Alpino), Localita' Rima, 8, 13026 Alto Sermenza, (VC), +39 0163 95001

Albergo Tagliaferro, double and twin rooms, wifi, SP10, 3, 13026 Rima, (VC), +39 333 888 5924

Rifugio Brusa (1km/15min south-west), mixed rooms, wifi, Alpe Brusà, 13029 Alto Sermenza, (VC), +39 346 634 7687

Albergo Nonaj (3km away but will provide shuttle), double and twin rooms, wifi, Localita' Piemoncucco, 1, 13026 San Giuseppe, (VC), +39 333 197 6614

Amenities

Meals and limited bar snacks available at accommodation providers.

Restaurant Grillo Brillo/Alpino in the centre of Rima.

Transport

None on route.

STAGE 12
Rima to Rifugio Valle Vogna

Start	Rima (1411m)
Finish	Rifugio Valle Vogna (1380m)
Distance	15.25km
Ascent	1220m
Descent	1270m
Time	6hr 45min

A straightforward stage ascending to the pass at Colle Mud beneath the towering cliffs of Monte Tagliaferro. Here the GTA passes close to the Monte Rosa massif. A further 500m ascent to the peak of Corno Mud provides, on a clear day, a stunning view of the mountain. The descent into Val Sesia and through Alagna does entail some road walking, but also the opportunity to pick up supplies and access other town resources.

From the main square in **Rima** return to the GTA-marked lane and turn left following the old street between closely set Walser houses, beautifully kept and adorned with begonias, neatly stacked firewood ageing below sheltered balconies once used to dry hay. The markings guide you to cross a bridge, then keeping right at the fork, begin the ascent through larch woodland, weaving back and forth on successive switchbacks. As you leave the trees behind, pass through the huts of Valmontasca (1821m) set among a carpet of alpenrose and bilberry. After a further 1km you pass more huts at **Alpe Vorco** (2076m) and the opportunity to refill water bottles at the piped spring. The way now becomes increasingly rocky and what remains of the Torrente Valmontasca on your left is lost beneath the boulders and scree as you reach **Colle Mud** (2324m).

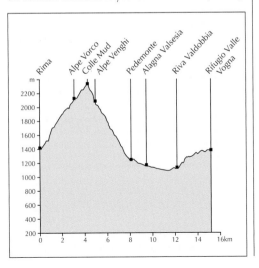

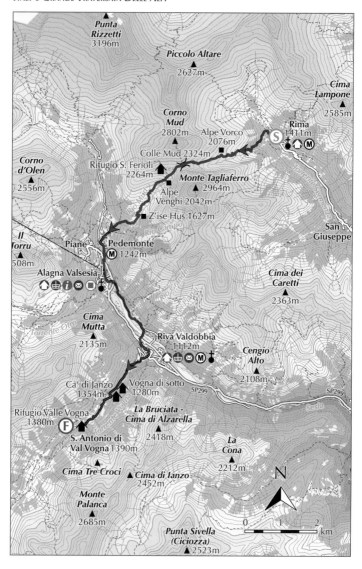

MONTE ROSA

In English the name Colle Mud can seem somewhat inappropriate as the terrain at the pass is invariably dry and stony, mud is little in evidence at all, but then of course mud has an entirely different meaning in Italian, actually meaning 'mount'. The mount in question lies to your right, Corno (meaning 'horn') Mud (2802m). From here on a clear day, uninterrupted views can be had of Monte Rosa's impressive main peaks and ridges. There can scarcely be a better position from which to admire or photograph Monte Rosa. There is a faint track from just beyond the *colle*, marked occasionally with cairns. However, the ascent is more or less straight up north-north-west and a 478m climb over two-thirds of a kilometre.

In this context 'Rosa' actually means 'glacier' in a local dialect, rather than 'pink' as one might expect. Until 1822 this was the only name given to the massif as a whole. At that time, Austrian cartographer Ludwig Freiherr von Welden sought to identify each of the nine discreet peaks of the massif by naming them (from left to right): Punta Giordani, Vincentpyramid, Schwarzhorn, Ludwighohe (his own name of course), Parrotspitze, Signalkuppe, Zumsteinspitze, Hochste Spitze (highest peak) and Nordend. Only Hochste Spitze was later renamed as Dufourspitze. Recorded attempts to climb Monte Rosa began as early as 1778. While von Welden reached the peak that subsequently bears his name in 1822, it was not until 20 years later in 1842 that the highest summit now known as Dufourspitze was conquered by the local parish priest Don Giovanni Gnifetti and seven companions on their fourth attempt.

From the *colle*, the descent to Valsesia begins gradually bearing south-west. A side track on your right leads to **Rifugio S. Ferioli**. Pass a succession of summer huts; **Alpe Venghi** (2042m), Alpe Mud di Mezzo (1895m), a small farm with drinking water and **Z'ise Hus** (1627m). On the final stretch into **Pedemonte** (1242m) a series of stone steps lead through woodland alongside the Rio Mud, which is then crossed to the south bank, shortly before the track becomes paved and the first traditional Walser houses appear on your left, high on terraced slopes. Follow the road down and cross the river, then turn left and continue down the hill into **Alagna Valsesia** (1191m).

Many modernised Walser houses are now summer homes

PEDEMONTE AND ALAGNA

Pedemonte is the oldest Walser settlement in the valley, first settled in the 12th century. The village houses outstanding examples of Walser homes and is largely untainted by more modern structures. The Walser Museum here occupies a 17th-century house, and is worth a visit if you are interested in understanding more about the Walser history and way of life.

Alagna offers the opportunity not only for more luxurious accommodations and a range of restaurants, supplies and a post office, but also the opportunity for one or more interesting side excursions. Your starting point for exploring these options will be the tourist office in the Piazza Grober in the centre of the small town. If you did not have the opportunity to view Monte Rosa from Corno Mud then you can take a shuttle bus from Alagna to the head of the valley and the Cascata dell Acqua Bianca, an impressive waterfall from where you stand below and can view the massive, sheer southern walls of the mountain. Alternatively, a gondola can whisk the visitor higher up onto the mountain to the foot of the glaciers below the breathtaking Punta Giordani (4046m).

On maps the route out of Alagna is the main road south-east for 2km. A considerably more pleasant alternative can be picked up from the main car park and bus terminus. Follow the road south-east for a short way until it curves away from the river where a footbridge across can be taken to the east bank. Turn immediately right and continue SE for a more pleasant 2km alongside the river. The track becomes paved at the small village of Balma (1104m) where at the junction take the right turn crossing the bridge, then cross the main road and take the slight left, uphill. The official route bypasses the main square of **Riva Valdobbia** (1112m) in favour of the switchbacks that climb above it, but a small detour into the pretty square with a water fountain and impressive frescos is worth taking. Red/White trail markings are largely absent from this stretch, nonetheless the route is straightforward now following the initial switchbacks uphill and small road all the way to **Sant' Antonio di Val Vogna** and **Rifugio Valle Vogna** (1380m) alongside the chapel. ▸

Beyond the church and water fountain in Riva Valdobbia an old steep mulatteria avoids retracing your steps and shortcuts the switchbacks to re-join the road higher up.

Incredible frescoes on the church at Riva Valdobbia

The **fresco** on the façade of the parish church in Riva Valdobbia depicts the Guidizio Universale (The Last Judgement). Painted by Tanzio, Melchiorre d'Enrico (son of Enrico) in 1596–97, this is perhaps the most famous work of art in the whole of Valsesia. Alongside it the gigantic image of S. Cristoforo, was believed to have been painted by Tanzio's brother Giovanni, both painters from Alagna.

FACILITIES INFORMATION FOR STAGE 12

Accommodation

Rifugio S. Ferioli, dormitory, Alpe Mud Di Sopra, 13021 Alagna Valsesia, (VC), +390163 91207

Agriturismo Alagna, double and twin rooms, wifi, Frazione Rusa, 13021 Alagna Valsesia, (VC), +39 328 963 1049

Residence Indren Hus, double and twin rooms, wifi, Via dei Walser, 18, 13021 Alagna Valsesia, (VC), +39 0163 91152

Albergo Monte Rosa, double and twin rooms, wifi, Piazza degli alberghi, 12, 13021 Alagna Valsesia, (VC), +39 0163 923209

B&B Tre Alberi Liberi, double and twin rooms, wifi, Via Nicolao Sottile, 7, 13021 Riva Valdobbia, (VC), +39 349 517 6388

Rifugio Valle Vogna, mixed rooms, Frazione S, Antonio 1, 13020 Riva Valdobbia, (VC), +39 0163 91918

Amenities

Meals and limited bar snacks available at accommodation providers except B&Bs.

A good variety of shops and restaurants are available in Alagna.

Transport

Alagna provides excellent transport connections. Two main bus lines connect Alagna with Novara and Milan on one, and Vercelli on the other. Both of these connect to train stations for onward travel. Bus tickets can be bought in Alagna from any tobacconist.

STAGE 13

Rifugio Valle Vogna to Rifugio Rivetti

Start	Rifugio Valle Vogna (1380m)
Finish	Rifugio Rivetti (2201m)
Distance	14.5km
Ascent	1250m
Descent	435m
Time	6hr

A large part of this stage follows the Torrente Vogna, essentially all of the way to the first pass. The climb is gradual until a couple of steeper sections later in the stage. You may be able to purchase a simple lunch at Alpe Maccagno before emerging among the rocky high peaks to spectacular panoramic views including a brief foray into the corner of the Aosta Valley before arriving at the ever-characterful Rifugio Rivetti.

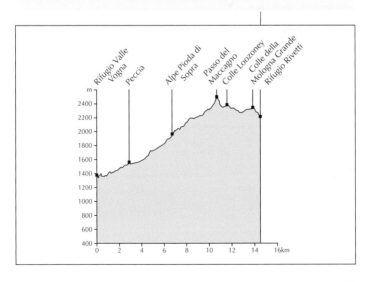

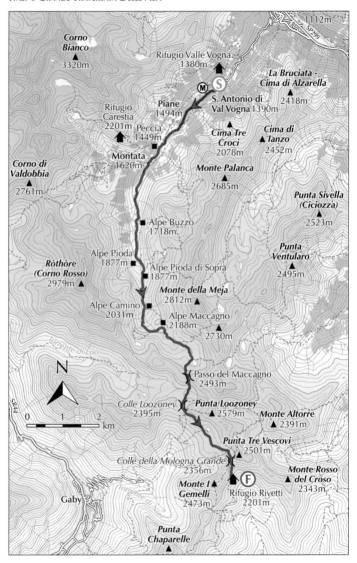

Corno
Bianco
3320m

Rifugio Valle Vogna
1380m

1112m

SP299

La Bruciata -
Cima di Alzarella

M S

S. Antonio di
Val Vogna 1390m

2418m

Piane
1494m

Rifugio
Carestia
2201m

Peccia
1449m

Cima Tre
Croci
2078m

Cima di
Tanzo
2452m

Montata
1620m

Monte Palanca
2685m

Corno di
Valdobbia
2761m

Punta Sivella
(Ciciozza)
2523m

Alpe Buzzo
1718m

Ròthòre
(Corno Rosso)
2979m

Alpe Pioda
1877m

Alpe Pioda di Sopra
1877m

Punta
Ventularo
2495m

Monte della Meja
2812m

Alpe Camino
2031m

Alpe Maccagno
2188m

2730m

Torrente di Loo

N

0   1   2
|_____|_____|
        km

SR44

Passo del Maccagno
2493m

Colle Loozoney
2395m

Punta Loozoney
2579m

Monte Altorre
2391m

Punta Tre Vescovi
2501m

Colle della Mologna Grande
2356m

Monte Rosso
del Croso
2343m

Monte I
Gemelli
2473m

F

Rifugio Rivetti
2201m

Torrente di Niel

Gaby

Punta
Chaparelle

Leaving the **Rifugio Valle Vogna** at S. Antonio, turn left and proceed up the gentle track alongside the Torrente Vogna. At one time a stone *mulattiera*, the track was widened for modern motor vehicles as far as the Walser settlement of **Peccia** (1449m) where the road ends and the path continues to the right, climbing through the scattered houses past the chapel. Beyond the chapel, cross the tributary by the stone napoleon bridge and then turn immediately left crossing the Torrente Vogna to the east bank where you turn right and continue on the bank above the *torrente*. This long, steady climb continues through grazing pasture, up the valley and past several *alpe* huts until **Alpe Pioda di Sopra** (1877m) where you cross to the west bank of the *torrente* (now more of a trickle) once more. What markings there were have now become quite faded, but the path picks a route up to the right of the valley, around a prominent 'knoll' to the broad plateau at **Alpe Maccagno** (2188m). ▶

The stone bridge in Peccia is known as the Ponte Napoleonico and was erected by French soldiers in 1800.

The summer **dairy farm** at Alpe Maccagno remains operated in the traditional way by the third generation of the same family producing the eponymous cheese by hand, which is matured on site. The family will, on request, sell cheese along with a simple lunch and wine for a small fee. Basic bunks in the hayloft may even be an option if it is late.

From the *alpe*, the indistinct path passes to the right of the lake and continues to climb south-east following a few small cairns, always staying close to what remains of the *torrente*, to the head of the valley at Lago Nero (tempting for a dip on a warm day), then climbs steeply up the right side of the valley wall, over boulders and scree, to the **Passo del Maccagno** (2493m). The initial short descent here is steep and requires care, particularly if wet, and you will want your hands free to guide you down. However, this soon levels out to cross a plateau before reaching the **Colle Loozoney** (2395m). Here you cross out of Piemonte momentarily and across a small corner of Valle d'Aosta. As you do so follow the markings

Rifugio Rivetti sits just below Colle della Mologna Grande at 2201m

to the left keeping to the high ground below the ridge, well above the summer farms below. Soon after Lago di Zuckie the path, although now distinct, crosses boulders once more in the ascent to the third and final pass of the stage at **Colle della Molongna Grande** (2356m). It is now just a short descent (returning into the Piemonte region) to **Rifugio Rivetti** (2201m).

FACILITIES INFORMATION FOR STAGE 13

Accommodation
Rifugio Rivetti, mixed rooms, Mologna Di, 13811 Andorno Micca, (BI), +39 0152 476141

Amenities
Meals and limited bar snacks available at Rifugio Rivetti.

Transport
None on route.

STAGE 14

Rifugio Rivetti to S. San Giovanni

Start	Rifugio Rivetti (2201m)
Finish	Santuario San Giovanni (1020m)
Distance	14.5km
Ascent	600m
Descent	1755m
Time	6hr 15min

The descent to Piedicavallo is steep but easy to follow. However, here awaits a bar for refreshment, shade and a rest for the knees. A brief but steep climb to the Madonna della Neve follows. Beside this popular pilgrimage site, the Rifugio does a brisk trade in lunches. Behind the Rifugio those are not the owner's dogs occupying a generous enclosure, but Carpathian Wolves! The way is easier from here on as you descend to Rosazza followed by a gentler walk to a pilgrim's accommodation at the Santaurio San Giovanni.

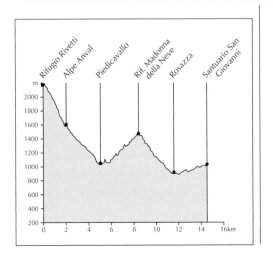

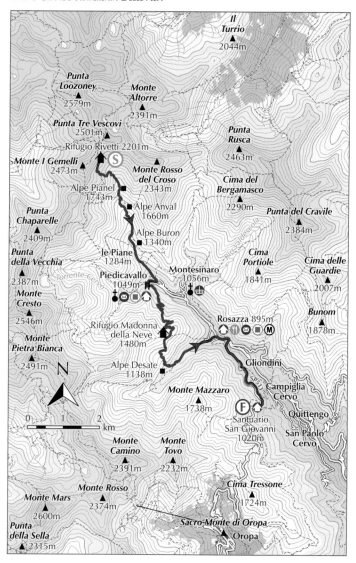

Il Turrio 2044m

Punta Loozoney 2579m

Monte Altorre 2391m

Punta Tre Vescovi 2501m

Rifugio Rivetti 2201m

Monte I Gemelli 2473m

Punta Rusca 2463m

Monte Rosso del Croso 2343m

Alpe Pianel 1743m

Cima del Bergamasco 2290m

Alpe Anval 1660m

Punta del Cravile 2384m

Alpe Buron 1340m

Punta Chaparelle 2409m

le Piane 1284m

Cima Portiole 1841m

Cima delle Guardie 2007m

Montesinaro 1056m

Punta della Vecchia 2387m

Piedicavallo 1049m

Monte Cresto 2546m

Rosazza 895m

Bunom 1878m

Rifugio Madonna della Neve 1480m

Monte Pietra Bianca 2491m

Gliondini

Alpe Desate 1138m

N

Monte Mazzaro 1738m

Campiglia Cervo

0   1   2
km

Quittengo

Santuario San Giovanni 1020m

San Paolo Cervo

Monte Camino 2391m

Monte Tovo 2232m

Cima Tressone 1724m

Monte Mars 2600m

Monte Rosso 2374m

Sacro Monte di Oropa

Punta della Sella 2315m

Oropa

102

Leaving **Rifugio Rivetti** take the path south-west, descending gently, initially in line with the ridge before turning sharply south-east, down the slope on flag stones where switchbacks ease the steepness of the descent. Cross the Torrente Mologna close to Alpe Pianel (1743m) and continue in descent on a well-marked path with the *torrente* always now on your right. The route is straight-forward into **Piedicavallo** (1049m), keep left where you descend between buildings and down steps to the awaiting bar, opposite the church.

At the bottom of the steps turn right, with the church on your right walk to the end of the road where a sign below a noticeboard guides you left, descending a little, across the sports ground to a stone bridge, and over the *torrente*. Follow a good path now into woodland and turn south-east to begin the climb. As the path steepens good use of switchbacks is made to reduce fatigue. Emerging onto the summit from under the cover of the trees into the light, you are surrounded by views in all directions, and probably more than ready for refreshment at the **Rifugio Madonna delle Neve** (1480m).

To continue, cross the *colle* (left out of the *rifugio*) and a clear path south-west leads past a small settlement at Alpe Vernetto. On the right side of the path here a piped spring provides an opportunity to collect water for the way ahead. Descend through deciduous woodland unexpectedly discovering the delightful and well-kept hamlet of **Alpe Desate** (1138m). The path from here into Rosazza follows an old *mulattiera*. Sadly, this has not been maintained and only the heavier flagstones remain, now standing proud of the surrounding ground that has since eroded. As the path emerges from the trees and becomes paved on the outskirts of **Rosazza** (895m), follow the road straight down the hill (past an unusual folly tower) to the t-junction where you turn right. All that remains now is a 3km stroll up a gentle gradient. After a short section of road, at **Gliondini** (also referred to as Jondini) the GTA is signposted through this small hamlet and onto an ancient pilgrimage trail, parallel to the road for much of the remaining way. The path

Mulattiera descending to Rosazza

emerges onto the road once more and directly ahead of you is rest and a bed for the night at the **Santaurio San Giovanni** (1020m).

Along the trail leading up to **Santaurio San Giovanni**, various information boards identify and explain sites of religious interest such as small chapels and shrines that were important to the pilgrims that travelled here.

ROSAZZA – THE VILLAGE GUIDED BY THE SPIRITS

In Valle Cervo, near Biella, among the mountains, lies the village of Rosazza, believed to be the most mysterious village in Italy. It takes its name from Federico Rosazza who brought great economic development to the community near the end of the 19th century.

During his long life, Federico suffered two devastating experiences, the premature death of his wife and that of his only daughter. This prompted him to explore the world of the occult, accompanied by his inseparable friend Giuseppe Maffei. It seems that both were convinced that their choices were guided by superior entities, and rumour has it that they often called upon the spirits for advice on the reconstruction of buildings in the village. The Parish Church was built on top of the old cemetery, which was moved to the opposite side of the River Cervo, and connected to the village by a bridge decorated with crosses and five-pointed stars. The church interior is completely painted dark blue and decorated with thousands of stars. The parish square leads into the municipal park, decorated with columns and a stone bear, which observes, not far away, a stone slab carved with an enigmatic inscription in runic letters, which no one has ever been able to decipher.

In addition to the Castle, the Church and the Cemetery, Federico commissioned the construction of numerous stone fountains along the village streets. Each one is different from the others, but they are all marked with recurring symbols, the rose and the five-pointed star. In the cobbled paving outside the cemetery, "stone tears" are distributed around the benches, representing pain, a symbol that often recurs in Masonic lodges.

FACILITIES INFORMATION FOR STAGE 14

Accommodation

Albergo Bar Ristorante Rosa Bianca, double and twin rooms, wifi, Via Roma, 10, 13812 Piedicavallo, (BI), +39 0156 09100

Rifugio Madonna della Neve (formerly known as Rifugio Sella), mixed rooms, Selle Di, 13815 Rosazza, (BI), +390156097000

Affittacamere La Valligiana, double and twin rooms, wifi, Via Federico Rosazza, 1, 13815 Rosazza, (BI), +39 338 655 0553

Santaurio San Giovanni, dormitory and rooms, wifi, Santuario, 13812 Campiglia Cervo, (BI), +39 0156 0006

Amenities

Meals and limited snacks available at accommodation providers.

A grocery store is available in nearby Montesinaro (1km/15min).

The rustic Autobahn bar/café in Rosazza (straight across the footbridge before you turn right) is highly recommended for lunch.

Transport

A regular bus service connects Piedicavallo with Biella (around 45min), a full-service town with a railway station for supplies or onward travel.

STAGE 15
S. San Giovanni to S. di Oropa

Start	Santuario San Giovanni (1020m)
Finish	Santuario di Oropa (1180m)
Distance	7.25km
Ascent	590m
Descent	465m
Time	3hr 30min

This short stage invites lingering to enjoy spectacular views. As you climb the whole of the Valle Cervo opens up below you, along with views out of the mountains to the plains of the Po Valley. The climb follows the narrow road up steep switchbacks and what traffic you see is consequently quite slow moving. The effort is highly rewarded at the quirky Locanda Galleria Rosazza where refreshment can be taken on a terrace with a panoramic outlook. Whether you choose to follow the path over the *colle*, or cut through the tunnel to the far side, the descent to Oropa is a simple path through woodland with glimpses of the great dome of the Santuario Oropa through the trees.

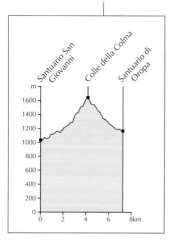

Leave the courtyard at **Santuario San Giovanni**, pass through the arched entrance gate and out onto the road. Turn left here, under a short tunnel and then uphill around the side of the building. At a fork keep left on the lower road through the pretty hamlet of Bele, re-joining the main road further up. At the first of several switchbacks, take the track left through houses to shortcut a couple of switchbacks. The climb becomes steeper now as you follow the switchbacks back and forth up the hillside, pausing regularly to enjoy the view. Several steep shortcuts across corners can be taken. Soon after the houses at Alpe del Caplun and Alpe

Testette, the road straightens, and you leave the trees behind. It is here that a small (easily missed) GTA sign marks where the path leaves the road on your right and climbs to the Alpe le Selle d'Oropa, before turning south and crossing to the **Colle della Colma** (1622m) on the main ridge below the peak of Cima Tressone (1724m). If you are planning on taking a well-earned break at the **Locanda Galleria Rosazza** (1485m) then ignore the path for the time being and continue up the road for a further 5min where this unique building, dating from 1897 and built by Federico Rosazza, occupies a prime viewpoint.

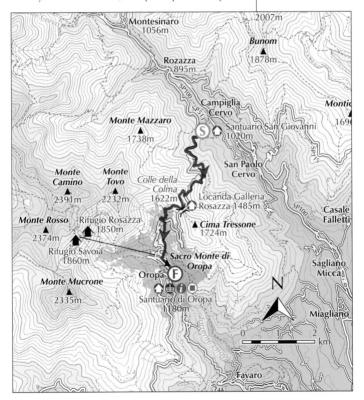

The quirky Locanda Galleria Rosazza

In the intervening years since the route of the GTA became established, the track up to the **Galleria Rosazza tunnel**, that was once closed to motor vehicles, became paved and open to traffic. This tunnel below Colle della Colma connects the Cervo valley to Oropa, as well as becoming an extension of the 'Strada Panoramica Zegna'. As a result, the climb is now shared with traffic, although it is usually only busy during the August holidays. There is an alternative (and largely level) route known as the Alta Via della Feda. This can be taken between San Giovanni and Oropa if you prefer (the route is displayed on a board at San Giovanni). However, the climb to the Colle della Colma is highly recommended for the panoramic views, as well as the visit to the unique and fascinating Locanda Galleria Rosazza (where lunch can include Sicilian specialities). The approach into Oropa from above also allows a perspective of the scale and layout of this famous site that cannot be gained from the valley.

From the Locanda Galleria Rosazza you can choose to take a shortcut through the galleria tunnel itself, or return to the path to climb over the *colle*. Taking the 355m long tunnel, hewn from the rock under the Colle della Colma, can be an adventure, but ensure you have a good torch. The tunnel is single track, unpaved and completely dark and you may encounter a car or motorbike. A short path on the far side reconnects with the GTA trail from the *colle*. The *colle* lies almost directly above the tunnel and is marked with a cross. The descent from the *colle* contours west initially below the Cima Tressone (1724m), then bears left more steeply downhill through switch-backs, joining with the track from the tunnel. A lovely section through deciduous woodland now ensues, offering tantalizing glimpses of Oropa through the trees. Cross the road from the *colle* part-way down and then continue down through woodland to emerge on a corner of the road near the shrine to Saint Eusebio. Continue straight ahead now, crossing the small bridge over the Torrente Oropa to arrive at the **Santuario di Oropa** (1180m).

FACILITIES INFORMATION FOR STAGE 15

Accommodation
Santuario di Oropa, mixed rooms, Via Santuario, 480, 13900 Oropa, (BI), +3901525551200

Amenities
Excellent meals and snacks provided at Locanda Galleria Rosazza.

Several good restaurant options around Oropa.

An excellent, if small mini-market in the main complex at Oropa will also provide sandwiches and panini. A larger market can be accessed by bus around 5km away in Favaro.

Transport
Bus 360 runs regularly between Oropa and Biella where onward connections can be made by train.

STAGE 16
S. di Oropa to Trovinasse

Start	Santuario di Oropa (1180m)
Finish	Trovinasse (1435m)
Distance	18km
Ascent	1450m
Descent	1180m
Time	7hr 45min

Leaving the busy Oropa behind, this stage among peaks and ridges will have you reaching for the camera on more than one occasion. Early morning mists shroud the valleys and lend a real mountaineering feel to the stage. Views stretch as far as the Matterhorn, while closer at hand you encounter the rocky lower slopes of the mighty Mont Mars. A pause for refreshment at the historic Rifugio Coda is not to be missed, with its memorabilia from the Tor de Geants, before lofty ridges take you out of the Biella Alps subgroup and into the gentler pastures of the lower Aosta Valley.

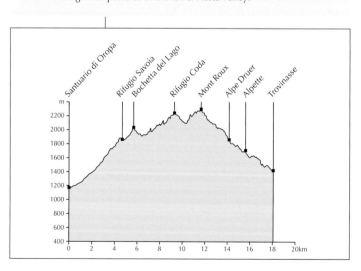

Steep protected sections on the way to Rifugio Coda

Many will take the cable car, but if you are walking up to the Rifugio Savoia (1860m) at the head of the cable car, then an early start is recommended to ascend before the sun gets too hot. Just upstream of the bridge you crossed yesterday on your way into Oropa, the road crosses back over the Torrente Oropa. On the far side, on your left, a clear path is signposted GTA. Take this path west alongside the *torrente*, gently uphill for 1km to where it joins the wider track. Continue up the track for a further 5min until you cross a tributary stream. Immediately after this turn right, passing *alpe* huts, and begin the steeper section of the climb, ascending the switchbacks below the cable car. At 1850m you pass below the **Rifugio Rosazza**, and just a few minutes further on at 1860m the **Rifugio Savoia**, where you may well want to rest a while in the busy bar, smug at your achievement among those who took the easy way up!

When you are ready to continue, follow the main track south-west, gently uphill, past the Lago del Mucrone (1894m) and on over the *colle* at **Bocchetta del Lago** (2026m). Ignoring side paths left (unless you are tempted by an excursion for the views from Monte

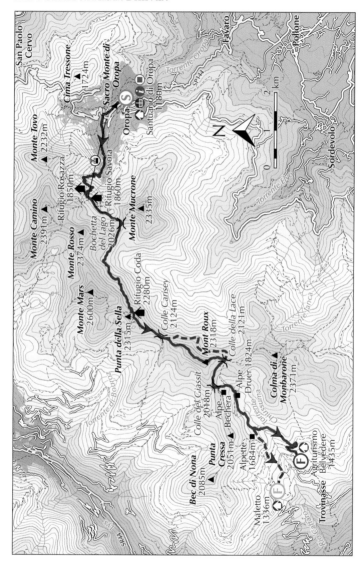

Mucrone), bear right and descend a short way, continuing past huts at Alpe Chardon (2011m) under the imposing south-east face of Monte Mars (2600m). Continuing around the slope the way becomes narrower now and rocky, more exposed sections are protected by a series of ropes and chains. The way is never difficult here but the added protection certainly gives confidence when the ground is wet. As you emerge onto leveller ground the path forks, keep left here and just around the corner you will find **Rifugio Coda** (2280m).

RIFUGIO CODA

Rifugio Coda is a popular staging point on the infamous 330km Tor de Geants (tour of the giants) mountain ultra-marathon. The event attracts some of the toughest ultra-distance runners from around the world and, unlike most events, has no compulsory stages, the clock is ticking regardless of rest breaks so the quickest overall route completion wins. Signed memorabilia from previous year's contestants can be found around the rifugio to the extent that it has become somewhat of a showcase for the event.

If you are curious about the line of large preserving jars found above the bar, apparently containing small cubes in liquid, this is the other thing that Coda is well known for: Zuccherino – flavoured sugar cubes suspended in exceptionally strong alcohol that prevents them from dissolving. These are not for the faint-hearted and the clove-flavoured cubes are particularly eye-watering. Perhaps this is the secret to surviving the gruelling Tor de Geants race!

If time allows, take a short walk to the summit of Punta della Sella (2315m), directly behind Rifugio Coda, for spectacular 360-degree views. From here both Monte Rosa and the Matterhorn are visible on a clear day.

Leaving Rifugio Coda, head south-west along a broad ridge line with occasional blazes on stones until the ridge begins to narrow and a small cross marks the **Colle Carisey** (2124m). Here the original GTA route (still marked as such on most maps) veers left below the east side of the ridge for around 1km to re-join the ridge at Colle della Lace. Erosion has left the path undermined in places on steep slopes and it has become overgrown, making way-finding and travel more difficult. Most now

Sunrise viewed from Rifugio Coda

walk the alternate route straight along the ridge (marked yellow for the Aosta Valley Alta Via 1 route). A head for heights is required, although protection is provided by cables in many places. If you choose this way continue via the peaks of Mont Bechit (2320m) and **Mont Roux** (2318m) to the **Colle della Lace** (2121m), clearly marked with a stone obelisk.

If you have descended from the ridge, turn right at the *colle* (if you took the lower path below the ridge, then the *colle* is straight ahead) and continue on the well-trodden path, north-west towards the **Colle del Giassit** (marked with a memorial cross, 2018m). Markings are vague here but descend south to **Alpe Druer** (1824m) and pick up the vehicle track. Take this south-west down the valley and soon the familiar red/white blazes confirm your route.

At **Alpette** (1684m), take the path off the track to the left, at a signpost marked to Trovinasse. Descend to and cross the *torrente*, then continue across the hillside, passing to the rear of a hut as you start to descend into trees. Emerge from the trees at Alpe Pianmaglio and descend between low walls to the track. Turn right at the signpost here and follow the track. After 10min take a sharp left on a broad track downhill. After a couple of switchbacks arrive at **Agriturismo Belvedere** on the upper slopes of **Trovinasse**.

If you are staying at the recently refurbished **Maletto Posto Tappa** across the valley, continue ahead at Alpette. Where the main track takes a sharp right turn, follow a GTA sign indicating a small path ahead SW through trees. At a further sign for Trovinasse the path bears right (W) now across more open ground where a church spire comes into view, continue towards this where you will arrive at Maletto (1336m).

FACILITIES INFORMATION FOR STAGE 16

Accommodation

Rifugio Rosazza, mixed rooms, 13900 Biella, Province of Biella, (BI), +39 339 460 2133

Rifugio Savoia, mixed rooms, Frazione Oropa, 13900 Biella (BI), +39 015 849 5131

Rifugio Coda, mixed rooms, Colle, Via Carisey, 13814 Pollone (BI), +39 393 573 4010

Agriturismo Belvedere, mixed rooms, wifi, Regione Trovinasse, 10010, Settimo Vittone, (TO), +39 0125 658731

Locanda Ristoro Maletto, double and twin rooms, wifi, Maletto, 10010 Carema, (TO), +39 327 121 9725 or +39 320 909 2744 (recommends booking or enquiries by WhatsApp)

Amenities

Meals and limited snacks available at accommodation providers.

Transport

None on route.

STAGE 17

Trovinasse to Quincinetto

Start	Trovinasse (1435m)
Finish	Quincinetto (295m)
Distance	7km
Ascent	10m
Descent	1145m
Time	2hr 45min

A pleasant descent through open woodland and grassy slopes, among the scattered dwellings below Trovinasse. The path becomes a *mulattiera* on the lower stretches into Sengie, after which a series of paths and roads deliver you into Quincinetto, the lowest point on the trail before you descend to the sea.

If you have stayed at **Agriturismo Belvedere**, descend the track to a corner with views across the valley, and bear left directly across the front of a new building. Follow the trail blazes into trees and over two pretty arched stone bridges into the heart of **Trovinasse** and descend alongside the church.

If you had crossed the valley to accommodation at Maletto, the return path (854A) joins the GTA here from Maletto.

Turn left at the signpost in front of the church, descend rough steps, and on through a grazed area. Continue past further huts into more open ground, then bear right to descend along a line of telegraph poles. At the road corner turn left and take the grassy slope alongside trees, to picnic benches and a water fountain. Turn left down the road a short way, then take a marked track alongside a hut on

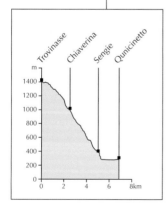

The path descends through grape vines

the right. Go straight across the next road, then at the next crossing, left for 100m and right onto the track once more. Pass a side turning for Settimo Vittone and continue downhill following marked blazes.

At the road entering **Sengie**, turn right, follow the road around the corner then at a signpost, marked 'Torre Daniele 0.25', turn left. It feels distinctly like you are entering someone's garden here, but keep right and the path soon becomes clear. At the next road descend to a vine terrace and follow it along until a blaze marking steps. Turn left and descend to the road then continue out through **Torre Daniele** to the main road where a right and a subsequent left across the bridge will take you into **Quincinetto** (295m).

FACILITIES INFORMATION FOR STAGE 17

Accommodation

Nuovo Hotel Tripoli, double and twin rooms, wifi, Strada Statale 26 della Valle, 57, 10010 Settimo Vittone, (TO), +39 0125 757608

B&B Le Rane, double and twin rooms, wifi, via circonvallazione, Frazione Torre Daniele, 49, 10010 Settimo Vittone, (TO), +39 328 625 2557

B&B Casa Val, double and twin rooms, wifi, Via Val, 8, 10010 Quincinetto, (TO), +39 347 680 5315

Mini Hotel, double and twin rooms, Via Umberto, 5, 10010 Quincinetto, (TO), +39 351 934 1104

Amenities

Meals and snacks available at Nuovo Hotel Tripoli.

Several restaurants and shops in Quincinetto.

Transport

Quincinetto no longer has a railway station. Take Bus 265 from Largo Europa (opposite the petrol station) to Pont Saint Martin train station. Bus tickets can be purchased in advance from the stationary shop round the corner on Via Stazione. From there the train to Milan Central takes around 2hr 20min, or to Turin (Porta Nuova) around 1hr 10min.

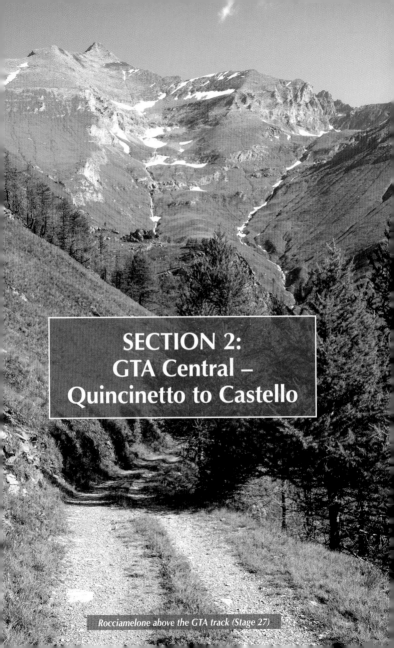

SECTION 2:
GTA Central –
Quincinetto to Castello

Rocciamelone above the GTA track (Stage 27)

SECTION 2:
GTA Central – Quincinetto to Castello

Distance	282.5km
Ascent	23,215m
Descent	21,920m
Maps	IGC Nos 3, 2, 1 & 6, 1/50k; NatGeo GTA 2 Centro 1/25k; Fraternali Editore Nos 5, 1 & 2, 1/50k
Stages	19

Overview

The central section of the route covers 19 stages from Quincinetto on the south-east corner of the Aosta Valley to Castello at the upper end of the Valle Varaita. Crossing first to the edge of the Gran Paradiso National Park, now in the Graian Alps, then heading west along the Valle di Locana to the Lago di Ceresole, the route then drops south close to the French border (a short way from the Vanoise on the French side) to skirt the slopes of the great pilgrimage mountain of Rocciamelone. From here you descend into the historic town of Susa, the largest settlement visited on the route and almost exactly halfway through the entire route, making it the obvious break point if you wanted to undertake the whole route in two trips.

Continuing south, the route crosses into the Cottian Alps and follows the edge of the Orsiera Rocciavré Parc to Usseaux, considered one of the most beautiful villages in Italy, and on to the headwaters of the Valle Pellice on the very edge of the French border and the Parc du Queyras. The final stages of this section see you step over the source of the great Po River, then cross the Monte Viso massif before descending to the head of Valle Varaita at the Lago di Castello.

To Quincinetto

Quincinetto no longer has a railway station so it is necessary to take the train to Pont Saint Martin, then get bus 265 from Piazza IV Novembre, to Quincinetto, Largo Europa (opposite the petrol station). The train to Pont

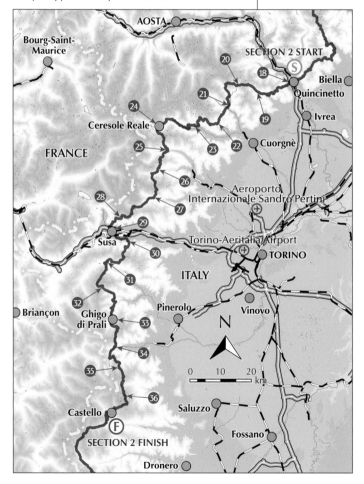

Saint Martin from Milan Central takes around 2hr 20min, or from Turin (Porta Nuova), around 1hr 10min.

From Castello
For onward travel from Castello you must first take a bus to Saluzzo. The bus runs from Pontechianale, through Castello to Casteldelfino, Sampeyre and then Saluzzo three times a day (more frequent in school term times), taking about 1hr 15min. Connections from Saluzzo include bus to Turin, taking about 1hr 20min, with Milan a further 50min by train.

STAGE 18
Quincinetto to Fondo

Start	Quincinetto (295m)
Finish	Fondo (1062m)
Distance	17.5km
Ascent	1975m
Descent	1195m
Time	8hr 30min

A steady climb from the trail's lowest point makes use of a remarkably good *mulattiera*, to Le Capanne, a good accommodation option for those wishing to break the stage here. Beyond, the trail climbs again to Alpe Chiaramonte, before descending to and along the Torrente Chiusella to reach the delightful hamlet at Fondo.

Leaving **Quincinetto**, climb up through the town, past the church then turn immediately right along a passage, Via Guglielmo Marconi. Follow this up through houses, bearing right into Via Cialdini then left into a lane that leads you first through vines then under trees, climbing steadily on a good *mulattiera*. Continue past an old

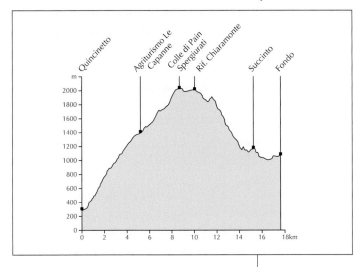

quartz quarry (497m) and across a track. An outcrop at a shrine provides an exceptional view across Quincinetto and the Doro Baltea river. At a small road corner, cross and continue, crossing the road a further five times before reaching the church and houses of **Santa Maria** (934m). Proceed uphill along the road to a corner and shrine, then turn left across the bridge and climb to re-join the road at a further corner. Keep left at the junction and continue uphill, after a short way leaving the road and crossing fields with sporadic trail blazes on rocks to reach a sign-post marked GTA. Take the left here, climb to the road and turn right to reach **Agriturismo Le Capanne** (1400m).

Take the small track that rises to the left of, and passes directly behind the buildings of Le Capanne. Keep the stream on your left initially and follow trail blazes across a cattle-grazed area. After a short distance, bear right to cross a further small stream, past a road hairpin and rise to the house and road at Cavanne (1567m). Continue uphill cutting across two road hairpins, then follow the road around the third hairpin before taking the track left off the road. From here follow the trail across a stream

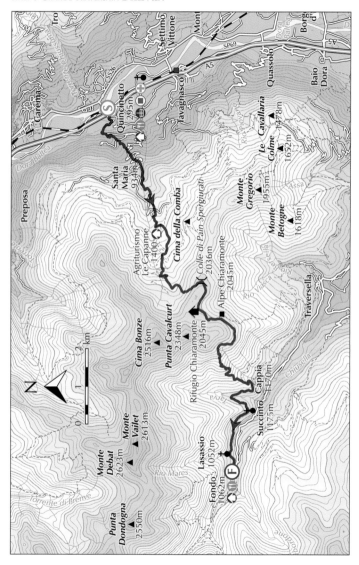

and uphill to the **Colle di Pain Spergiurati** (2036m). Cross the *colle* and contour around the hillside to reach the Rifugio and a little further on, **Alpe Chiaramonte** (2045m). ▶

Alternative accommodation off trail can be found at Rifugio Bruno Piazza (1050m) on the slopes above Travesella. Turn left on path 719 after Alpe Chiaramonte, returning on path 730 to Cappia.

> Giorgio and Maria Marino at **Alpe Chiaramonte** are somewhat legends of the trail, taking great delight in serving hikers with milk, cheese, yogurt and polenta, demonstrating their way of life and encouraging photographs.

From Chiaramonte, follow the contour south-west around the slope, on a narrow path that is at times unclear. Passing around the southern ridge of Punta Cavalcurt, bear north-west to reach the huts of Casa Binelli. Turning west here, descend steeply past the first huts, then to the huts at Ravissa (1670m), and pass below the prominent crag here to continue through switchbacks downhill. At **Cappia** (1170m) descend between houses, swinging left then right at the next and subsequent houses before the path forks. Keep right here, downhill to a viewpoint and shrine, then turn right to contour the gully of

Trattoria at Fondo behind the 17th-century bridge

the Torrente Tarva and reach the church and houses at **Succinto** (1175m). From here follow the easy, well-made path above the Torrente Chiusella, past old huts and a waterfall to reach **Fondo**. The *posto tappa* is at the foot of the bridge on the right.

> The elegant bridge at **Fondo**, dating from 1727, is one of seven remaining enlightenment-era arched stone bridges in the Valchiusella.

FACILITIES INFORMATION FOR STAGE 18

Accommodation

Agriturismo Le Capanne, dormitory and double rooms, wifi, Via XXV Aprile 4 – Reg. Cavanne, 10010 Quincinetto, (TO)

Rifugio Chiaramonte, dormitory (bed only, meals possible at *alpe* but phone in advance), Alpe Lavasoza, Travesella, TO, +39 338 276 4607

Posto Tappa GTA Trattoria del Ponte, double and triple rooms, Frazione Fondo, Travesella, (TO), +39 0125 749124

Alternative accommodation off trail on the slopes above Travesella at Rifugio Bruno Piazza, mixed rooms, Localita Pieuj, Travesella, (TO), +39 0125 749233, +39 346 626 9405. Accessed by turning left on path 719 after Alpe Chiaramonte, returning on path 730 to Cappia.

Amenities

Meals and limited snacks available at accommodation providers.

Transport

None on route.

STAGE 19

Fondo to Piamprato

Start	Fondo (1062m)
Finish	Piamprato (1550m)
Distance	11.75km
Ascent	1345m
Descent	865m
Time	5hr 45min

An exhilarating stage that starts gently, climbing alongside the *torrente* that alternates between burbling brook and deep, tranquil pools, before ascending more steeply to the *colle*. The descent into a dramatic gorge is aided by chains and ropes for short sections of exposed rock as you climb down alongside the cascade and plunging pools of Rio Giaset.

From **Fondo**, remain on the north bank and follow the Torrente Chiusella upstream. Initially among shaded woodland, the path is at times walled and weaves among ancient, mostly abandoned, buildings. Continue ahead past **Tallorno** (1225m), keeping to the right bank of the *torrente*. From here the track becomes less distinct but regular red/white blazes on rocks reassure the hiker. Heading for **Alpe Pasquere** (1486m), the path rises up the slope away from the *torrente*. Follow this directly between buildings alongside a cow shed bearing GTA marking. The path now becomes a clear vehicle

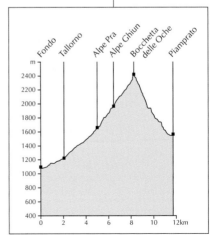

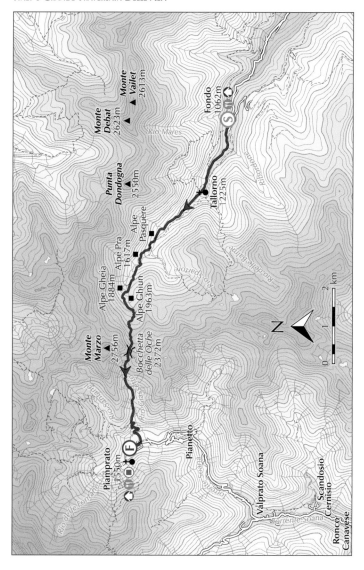

track for a way, passing one of the ancient arched stone bridges on your left. Continue ahead for a way, then leave the track before it crosses the *torrente*, on a path climbing more steeply now towards the summer farm at **Alpe Pra** (1617m).

Shortly after Alpe Pra, cross the *torrente*, turn right and continue to climb following red/white trail blazes on rocks. Follow this track back and forth across the upper tributaries of the *torrente* as you climb through successive *alpe* plains, each with a cluster of huts in various states of disrepair, eventually reaching the *colle* of **Bocchetta delle Oche** (2372m).

Descend west from the *colle* across initially grassy slopes into increasingly thick vegetation. Dominated by alder that conspires to conceal the footing, the way is difficult at times, crossing slabs of rock and descending small earthy chutes along the southern edge of a rushing gorge. Rope and chain, along with occasional metal rungs, are provided here in recognition of the challenge, and go some way to provide reassurance and a safe descent. Nonetheless, care is required, especially if it is

Rock fall across the path leaves a low passage way

The posto tappa Aquila Bianca at Piamprato is situated in the 19th-century former school house. A building that was bequeathed to the grateful inhabitants by the king.

wet. As the gradient eases, cross the *torrente* to the northerly bank and continue downhill. Surprisingly late-lying snow and ice are common here bridging the *torrente* out of reach of direct sunlight, and a small scramble up the slope may be required to bypass it. Descend through trees to meet a second stream and a dusty track dominated overhead by electricity pylons. Turn left here and descend, crossing a meadow to the road. Turn right, cross the bridge and into **Piamprato**. ◄

FACILITIES INFORMATION FOR STAGE 19

Accommodation

Posto Tappa GTA Aquila Bianca, mixed rooms, wifi, Frazione Piamprato, Valprato Soana, (TO), +39 0124 812993

Rifugio Ciavanassa (new in 2022), mixed rooms, wifi, Frazione Piamprato, Valprato Soana, (TO), +39 340 582 3775

Chalet Rosa dei Monti (previously Albergo Giaset), mixed rooms, wifi, Frazione Piamprato, Valprato Soana, 10080 (TO), +39 347 226 9040

Amenities

Meals and limited snacks available at accommodation providers.

Transport

A regular bus from Pont Canavese runs as far as Valprato Soano, and twice a day (morning and evening) extends to Piamprato. From Pont Canavese it is around 2hr by train to Turin.

STAGE 20

Piamprato to Ronco Canavese

Start	Piamprato (1550m)
Finish	Ronco Canavese (946m)
Distance	16.5km
Ascent	1475m
Descent	2090m
Time	8hr

The bus between Piamprato and Ronco has commonly been used here as the stage was closed for many years following floods and a devastating landslip. An alternative route has been adopted now, which allows a foray into the peaks of Italy's oldest national park, Gran Paradiso. It is worth noting, however, that it is less walked as other guide books haven't caught up yet. As a result, it is a little wilder and following the trail is a little tougher in a couple of places. Don't let that put you off however, it is a great hike with the convenience of a bridge across to a restaurant around half way, a perfect lunch spot.

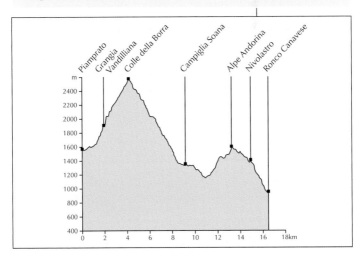

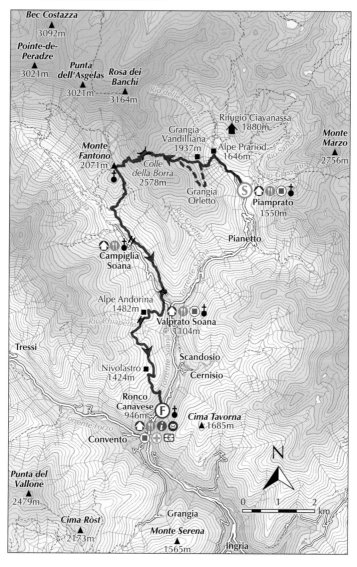

Bec Costazza
▲ 3092m

Pointe-de-
Peradze
▲ 3021m

Punta
dell'Asgelas
▲ 3021m

Rosa dei
Banchi
▲ 3164m

Rio delle Fontane

Rifugio Ciavanassa
▲ 1880m

Monte
Marzo
▲ 2756m

Grangia
Vandilliana
1937m

Alpe Prariod
1646m

Rio Santanel

Rio Giassetton

Monte
Fantono
▲ 2071m

Colle
della Borra
2578m

Grangia
Orletto

Piamprato
1550m

Rio Orleto

Pianetto

Campiglia
Soana

Torrente Soana

Alpe Andorina
1482m

Rio Chiapell

Valprato Soana
1104m

Tressi

Nivolastro
1424m

Scandosio

Cernisio

Torrente Soana

Ronco
Canavese
946m

Cima Tavorna
▲ 1685m

Torrente Forzo

Convento

N

Punta del
Vallone
▲ 2479m

Cima Ròst
▲ 2173m

Grangia

Monte Serena
▲ 1565m

Ingria

0   1   2
km

Leaving **Piamprato**, head north-west, through the village following GTA-marked signposts (yellow now, rather than the customary red/white, as you are in Parc Gran Paradiso) for Colle Borra. Follow the road as far as **Alpe Prariod** (1646m). Turn left here, crossing the stream and follow the track for a steady climb through grazing meadow and up into the trees. After a series of switchbacks, you emerge at **Grangia Vandilliana** (1937m) which occupies a shelf overlooking the valley. The signage here can be confusing. Many maps show the GTA turning left here to avoid a steep climb and traversing the slope on a good path via Grangia Orletto. Signs on the ground now take the more direct route up the steep slope behind Grangia Vandilliana. The former is undoubtedly the easier path, and around June–July the slopes around **Grangia Orletto** are awash with Rhododendron flowers too. Either are good options. If you opt for the direct climb, pass to the right of the huts and tackle the slope head on. Sporadic blazes on rocks are present but faint, and it is essentially a case of merely picking the best line and climbing until you re-join the more worn track from Grangia Orletto. Continue uphill to the small hut at Grangia della Borra

Passing the hut at Localita Pugnon

(2241m), then zigzag steeply up the gully of the Rio della Borra all the way to **Colle della Borra** (2578m).

> **Chamois and marmots** are a regular sight on either side of the *colle* from where there is a wonderful view over the Vallone di Campiglia and the peaks beyond.

Leave the *colle* on switchbacks that ease the gradient, weaving between small crags on the lower reaches. As the ground levels momentarily, turn left at a signpost just before the incongruous chapel at **Monte Fantono** (2071m), then continue down the gully of the upper reaches of the Rio Fanton, passing a couple of shrines. Pass behind the hut at Localita Pugnon (1630m) and descend south-east into trees to cross the stream and follow the path across damp meadow alongside the *torrente*. After a short distance, a footbridge on your right provides a route into **Campiglia Soana** (1345m). Continue along the footpath through trees keeping the *torrente* on your right. The path is vague at times through here until you reach Chiesale (1180m).

Descend the road to cross the bridge and rise to the main road. Here turn left then almost immediately take the signposted path right into the trees. Follow the track through the largely abandoned dwellings at **Alpe Andorina** (1482m) and below, the restored church of San Antonio. Follow the contour around then descend to the gully of the Rio Chiapetto where a wooden bridge enables an easy crossing. Climb steeply to a further recessed gully where metal rungs and chains provide confidence if it is wet. A gradual descent now ensues through woodland to reach **Nivolastro** (1424m), once entirely abandoned, now with some restoration. From here an old *mulattiera* eases the final descent into **Ronco Canavese**. ▸

An office of the Parc National Gran Paradiso is located in Ronco Canavese, including a visitor information centre.

FACILITIES INFORMATION FOR STAGE 20

Accommodation
Rifugio Ciavanassa (new in 2022), mixed rooms, wifi, Frazione Piamprato, Valprato Soana, (TO), +39 340 582 3775

Phoenix Hostel, mixed rooms, Strada Comunale, 10080 Campilgia Soana (TO), +39 0124 373288

Locanda Alpina, double/twin rooms, Frazione Bordone, 3, Valprato Soana, (TO), +39 0124 812929

Posto Tappa GTA B&B Gran Paradiso, Ronco Canavese, (TO), +39 366 260 9598

Albergo Centrale, mixed rooms, wifi, laundry, Via Roma 25, 10080 Ronco Canavese, (TO), +39 0124 817401

Amenities
Meals and limited snacks available at accommodation providers.

Restaurants at Campiglia Soana, Valprato Soana and Ronco Canavese.

Transport
A regular bus connects Ronco with Pont Canavese. From Pont Canavese it is around 2hr by train to Turin.

STAGE 21
Ronco Canavese to Talosio

Start	Ronco Canavese (946m)
Finish	Talosio (1227m)
Distance	10km
Ascent	1180m
Descent	905m
Time	4hr 45min

A simple stage that climbs steadily through woodland and pasture over the *colle* from the Val Soana into the Ribordone. Alongside extensive views and *alpe* huts, a highlight of the stage would surely be the inclusion of a stop at the fascinating 17th-century Santuario di Prascondu.

From the centre of **Ronco Canavese** take the road south-west, alongside the river and past the Santurio del Crest

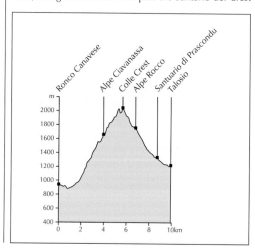

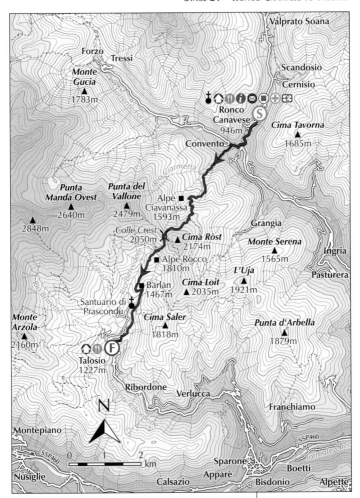

(896m). Cross the road bridge over the Torrente Forzo and turn immediately right by the bus stop. After a short walk along the road, and before the road fork, take the signposted track left. Ignore a further left and keep

Tracks can be obscured through grazing

ahead through the trees. Follow the track across the stream and continue the steady climb. Pass behind the hut at **Alpe Ciavanassa** (1593m) and a little further on pass between the cluster of huts at Alpe Sionei (1856m). Out of the trees now, cattle tracks can obscure the trail but faint blazes on sporadic rocks help to guide as you climb around 150m further before contouring right to reach **Colle Crest** (2050m). The trail from Ronco was ill-maintained and overgrown for many years. An alternative, still marked on many maps, left Val Soana through Bosco, following a small road south-east of Punta del Sionei, through Grangia to take path 611 and re-join the route at Colle Crest.

Descending from the *colle* to the huts at **Alpe Rocco** (1810m), cattle tracks can again obscure the trail but the open ground and line of sight prevent this from being an issue. Below Alpe Rocco continue down the increasingly narrow nose of the ridge under trees to a viewpoint, then take the path left off the ridge, steeply down under tree cover, before switching back south along the Rio Roc to reach the **Santuario di Prascondu** (1327m). From here follow the path south following waymarkers, crossing the Torrente Ribordone to reach a gravel car park and information board just outside **Talosio**. Turn left and head downhill to find the Trattoria where keys to the *posto tappa* can be obtained.

> The somewhat basic *posto tappa* at **Talosio** is up the hill in the old school building. Keys are held at the trattoria where a good breakfast and dinner are provided at a set rate.

SANTUARIO DI PRASCONDU

The construction of the Santuario di Prascondu is linked to a religious fact officially recognised by the Catholic Church. On 27th August 1619, an apparition of the Madonna appeared to a mute young Giovannino Berrardi, asking him to undertake a pilgrimage to Loreto, something his father had earlier vowed he would do. On the return journey Giovannino miraculously regained his speech. The initial chapel built on the site of the vision around 1620 was swept away by an avalanche a short time after its dedication in 1654. In 1659 the construction of a new church began and the current building remains with several additions and changes over the years.

FACILITIES INFORMATION FOR STAGE 21

Accommodation
Posto Tappa GTA Trattoria Grisolano, dormitory, Frazione Talosio, 46 Ribordone (TO), +39 0124 818015

Amenities
Meals and limited snacks available at accommodation provider.

Transport
None on route.

STAGE 22
Talosio to San Lorenzo

Start	Talosio (1227m)
Finish	San Lorenzo (1042m)
Distance	13km
Ascent	1370m
Descent	1545m
Time	6hr 30min

An exhilarating stage over high mountain paths and ridges with distant views. *Mulattiera* and good tracks are interspersed with a couple of trickier sections where care is needed over rock and scree. Marking is good, except perhaps for the descent from Alpe Praghetta, where occasional blazes of red/white paint on rocks are faded and sporadic.

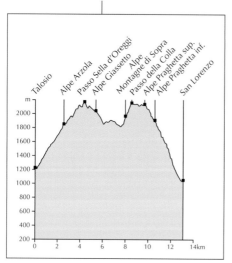

Follow the *mulattiera* up through **Talosio**, past a bar to the church and take the arch under houses to find the path to Posio. Follow this uphill under trees and across the road switchbacks then through the pretty houses of Frazione Posio (1327m). From here strike out west on a steady incline and good path under dense tree cover initially, thinning as you reach **Alpe Arzola** (1793m). Continue the climb to the ridge where you

find a signpost. Ignoring the track to Bivacco Blessant Redentore (1976m), turn right and ascend the ridge directly, passing just below the summit of Monte Arzola (2158m). Continue along the airy ridge, and over the **Passo Sella d'Oreggi** (2175m).

Once across and a little below the *colle*, turn north-west and descend across rocky and scrubby terrain towards the reservoir of Lago d'Eugio (1897m), passing the abandoned huts at **Alpe Giassetto** (2044m). It is necessary to climb down below the first section of dam wall, cross the outflow, then ascend steps to a level grassy area below a building on the rocky outcrop that sits midway across the reservoir wall. Pass behind the rock and then cross the second section of dam wall. Turn left now and follow the broad stony road south-west to **Alpe Montagne di Sopra** (1864m) where, after a couple of switchbacks take the signposted path on the right towards the *colle*. Climb steeply here over rock and scree to reach the **Passo della Colla** (2170m). At the pass, a fenced and well-maintained hut belongs to the

Blazes on rocks aid way-finding on the open hillside

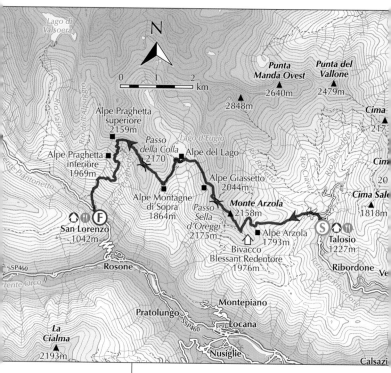

park authorities. A useful water tap can be found to the rear of the building.

> Constructed in the 1950s by the Italian Electricity Commission, the **dam** flooded the valley as part of a push to utilise the natural geography for hydro-electric power.

Continuing north-west, contour across the south-west flank of Punta di Praghetta (2386m), crossing several small tributaries of the Rio di Praghetta to reach the huts of **Alpe Praghetta superiore** (2159m). At the track junction here, turn left and begin the descent through successive switchbacks, down boulder-strewn slopes, to firstly **Alpe Praghetta inferiore** (1969m), (where a caravan is not only an incongruous sight, but raises the inevitable question of how it got there, halfway up the mountainside), then Alpe la Ca (1685m). Turn left between the old huts, marked by a footpath sign, then drop to the right once more as you descend below the treeline. After a short distance a ledge is reached with a fine view down the valley. The descent continues through trees, losing height quickly through tight switchbacks. At Ciadagn (1287m) pass a couple of houses on the left of the track. A short way beyond this keep left at the fork through Bouro, and then between houses entering **San Lorenzo** to the main road. Turn left for a short way downhill to the *trattoria*.

The **Trattoria di San Lorenzo** is a fantastic example of local enterprise. Simone Reale is a guide for the Gran Paradiso National Park as well as running the trattoria, which she describes as a farm, keeping a range of poultry, pigs, goats and growing produce of all kinds. She is an enthusiastic host and guests are treated to an incredible feast of sampling dishes and specialities which never seem to stop coming, many of which come from her own produce.

FACILITIES INFORMATION FOR STAGE 22

Accommodation

Bivacco Blessant Redentore, always open, 3 mattresses only, Alpe Arzola, Frazione Talosio, (TO), +39 015 60007

Trattoria San Lorenzo, 2 large shared rooms, Strada Comunale Rosone – Piantonetto, 10080 Locana, (TO), +39 0124 800213, +39 340 126 0343

Amenities

Meals and limited snacks available at accommodation provider.

Transport

None on route.

STAGE 23

San Lorenzo to Ceresole Reale

Start	San Lorenzo (1042m)
Finish	Ceresole Reale (1582m)
Distance	26km
Ascent	1935m
Descent	1465m
Time	10hr 45min

Traditionally this stage is broken into two, with a night at Noasca, and some may wish to do this. However, while the initial stage of the route via Meinardi and down to Fey is interesting, the long stretch up the valley on one side of the road or the other is somewhat tedious and provides little shade. On top of this the *posto tappa* at Noasca has been noted by many as consistently unwelcoming. A solution therefore is to walk the initial section in the morning, then take the bus to Noasca from Frazione Fornetti, which takes just six minutes, and walk the pleasant section from Noasca to Ceresole Reale in the afternoon, and if you have time, explore the Lago di Ceresole.

Bus from Frazione Fornetti to Noasca: GTT5137 at 10:59am – don't miss it, the next one is 14:58pm!

◀ Leave **San Lorenzo**, head south-east descending the road for some way, across the *torrente* and through the hamlet of Rocci (972m). Here the GTA path leaves the road at a signpost. Turn right and follow the track up through trees, passing hydro-electricity pipelines, and on past abandoned huts at Bertodasco (1917m). At **Perebella** take a sharp right uphill more steeply and climb to a level grassy terrace then follow the signpost guiding you left. This continues for some way before crossing a boulder field, then after a short further section of dense undergrowth arrive at the abandoned hamlet of **Meinardi** (1460m).

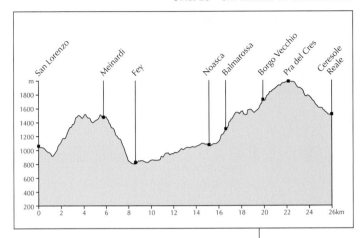

The shrine and chapel of **Sant'Anna at Meinardi** is remarkably well preserved despite the abandoned and decaying state of the dwellings around it. The ornate and decorative chapel was restored in 1891 by architect Camillo Boggio and is said to be a

The chapel of Sant'Anna di Meinardi

145

testimony to the neo-gothic and neo-romanesque styles of the late nineteenth century. Decorated with depictions of the saint, the chapel is the destination of an annual pilgrimage held on the last Sunday of each July.

Continuing beyond Meinardi, take a signposted path left after a short distance and descend an easy-to-follow track down through trees, passing huts at Casa Barrera (1251m) and Mesonette (1057m) before emerging onto a small road on the edge of **Fey** (826m). Turn right and proceed to the main road where (if not taking the bus), you cross the road and turn left before almost immediately

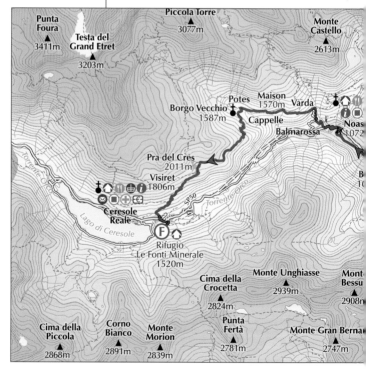

crossing the bridge and following the path to the right.
Cross back to the north side and turn left for **Frera inferiore** then superiore, then a further crossing to Jerener, past
the chapel and right up the valley once more. Continue
now through successive hamlets until you enter **Noasca**
(1072m).

Leave Noasca by the road which, after a couple of
switchbacks, heads west. At the first bus stop take the
signposted GTA path right, climbing quickly into the
trees then across the corner of the road at **Balmarossa**.
Continue uphill parallel to the *torrente*, bypassing the
road corners, then just beyond the car park at the top,
turn left. A succession of abandoned hamlets are passed

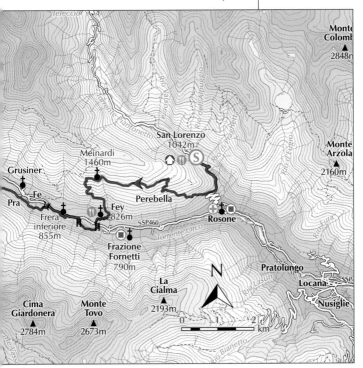

The path approaching Lago di Ceresole

now on the old path that traverses the slope through pasture. First **Varda** where the mule track is accompanied by 'hole-in-the-wall' shrines, then **Maison** with its old schoolhouse and tiny chapel, followed by **Cappelle** and finally **Potes**. From here take the path across the stream and past the old chapel at **Borgo Vecchio** (1587m), then bear left steeply uphill into trees. Climb steadily to undulating pasture occupied by inquisitive marmots, then at **Pra del Cres** (2011m) bear left and begin to descend once more. At Casa Bianca the path forks. Keep left and descend a broad woodland track down the flank of the hill towards **Ceresole Reale**. For Rifugio Le Fonti Minerale take the marked path left just above houses to descend to a hairpin in the road. Follow this through two bends then take a signed right down to and across the Torrente Orco where the rifugio is ahead.

FACILITIES INFORMATION FOR STAGE 23

Accommodation

Posto Tappa GTA Albergo Gran Paradiso, mixed rooms, Corso Umberto1, Noasca, (TO), +39 340 472 9334

Albergo Caccia Reale, double rooms, Via Roma, 14 Noasca, (TO), +39 0124 901128

Rifugio Le Fonti Minerali, mixed rooms, wifi, Borgata Fonti, 10080 Ceresole Reale (TO), +39 347 711 0309

Albergo Aquila Alpina, double and family rooms, wifi, Borgata Pian della Balma, 1, 10080 Ceresole Reale (TO), +39 339 824 0132

Ristorante Chalet del Lago, double and family rooms, wifi, Borgata Pian della Balma, 10, 10080 Ceresole Reale (TO), +39 012 495 3128

Albergo Meublè Sport di Moretti Daniela, double and family rooms, wifi, Borgata Capoluogo, 12, 10080 Ceresole Reale (TO), +39 349 293 5560

Ristorante Albergo Tre Levanne, double and family rooms, wifi, Borgata Capoluogo, 21, 10080 Ceresole Reale (TO), +39 012 495 3004

Amenities

Meals and limited snacks available at accommodation providers.

Restaurants, groceries, tourist office and post office available in Noasca and Ceresole Reale.

ATM also in Ceresole Reale.

Transport

Bus 5137 departs from Ceresole Reale three times a day for Pont Canavese (1hr), from where train can be taken to onward destinations.

STAGE 24
Ceresole Reale to Pialpetta

Start	Ceresole Reale (1582m)
Finish	Pialpetta (1050m)
Distance	12.5km
Ascent	1115m
Descent	1550m
Time	6hr

This stage is essentially a straightforward climb to a *colle*, and descent to Pialpetta. However, to describe it as such would miss the cascading waterfalls, the sweet scent of pine needles through the cool forest, the mystery of Piano dei Morti, the dramatic crags and spires around Colle della Crocetta and the flower-filled hanging valleys and pasture that encourage a lingering descent.

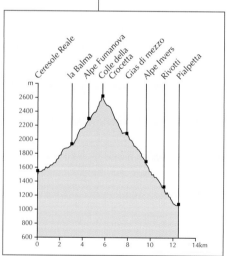

Commencing behind the historic *rifugio* of **Fonti Minerale**, climb the steep slope through trees to the south end of the dam wall. If you started from higher in the village, then a descent to the lake and crossing of the dam brings you to this point. Follow the path around the south side of the lake for around ten minutes to reach a clear track junction where the ascent begins.

Before the ascent, take a walk beyond the

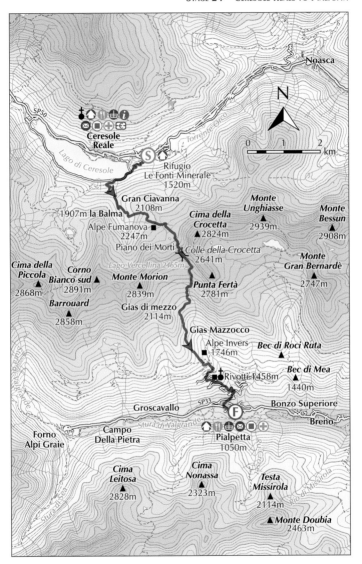

track junction to the **Cascata del Dres** which can be spectacular after wet weather, especially in the early autumn colours of September.

Turn left and begin to climb, gently at first, through pine and deciduous trees. After a couple of switchbacks turn more directly up the slope and follow the path of a stream, eventually crossing and climbing to the hut at **la Balma** (1907m). Surrounded by soft grasses and moss-covered rocks, bear left and continue to climb as the trees give way to open sky and the imposing grey wall ahead. Before long you ascend a scree-filled gully to the flat, stony plateau of **Piano dei Morti** (2363m).

> **Piano dei Morti** (plain of the dead) is not, as is common in mountains everywhere, a resting place on a 'coffin route' over a *colle* to a burial ground. Here it refers to the burial place of the victims of an appalling fight that broke out on this site in the 1800s over the theft of a church bell from Groscavallo in Val Grande, by some unprincipled residents of Ceresole Reale.

Colle della Crocetta 2641m

The final stages of the climb are a series of switch-backs up a steep rocky incline to reach the imposing crest of **Colle della Crocetta** (2641m). Descend south-east from the *colle*, initially over similarly steep terrain, but easing as you skirt left above Lago Vercellina. Sporadic blazes on rocks keep you easily on track as you descend grassy slopes past successive *alpe* huts and cross to the right side of Vallone di Vercellina. Continue downhill at the track junction at **Gias di mezzo** (2114m), eventually past **Alpe Invers** (1746m) to a track. Bear right here and shortcut a couple of road corners then bear right again to descend to the whitewashed church at **Rivotti** (1458m). Continue below the church, crossing the road to the right of houses, past a couple more houses and shrines to reach **Pialpetta**.

FACILITIES INFORMATION FOR STAGE 24

Accommodation

Posto Tappa GTA Albergo Setugrino, double rooms, wifi, (or keys for separate dormitory), Frazione Pialpetta, Groscavallo, (TO), +39 0123 81016

Albergo Pialpetta, double rooms, wifi, Piazza San Lorenzo, 1 Frazione Pialpetta, Groscavallo, (TO), +39 0123 81044

Amenities

Meals and limited snacks available at accommodation providers.

Restaurant, post office, pharmacy and groceries in Pialpetta.

Transport

A once daily bus runs from Pialpetta to Germagnano, where a train departs hourly for Turin airport.

STAGE 25
Pialpetta to Balme

Start	Pialpetta (1050m)
Finish	Balme (1426m)
Distance	15km
Ascent	1605m
Descent	1195m
Time	6hr 45min

Crossing from Valle Grande to Valle Ala, this stage is wonderfully varied with a wild and remote feel full of craggy outcrops, rich vegetation and glacial lakes. Mists can hang among the valleys making the crossing atmospheric. Way marking is mostly good, but dense vegetation can slow the hiker in places and may lengthen the time required.

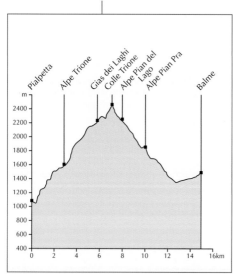

Leave **Pialpetta** east along the main road. As you cross into Migliere turn right, dropping to a bridge. Cross the Torrente Stura di Vallegrande here and, ignoring side tracks, continue ahead, then immediately keep right at the fork and climb into trees. The climb, while not difficult, can be narrow and overgrown on a sometimes-precipitous path above the valley requiring care and a little extra time. Beyond **Alpe Trione** (1648m) the terrain begins to change

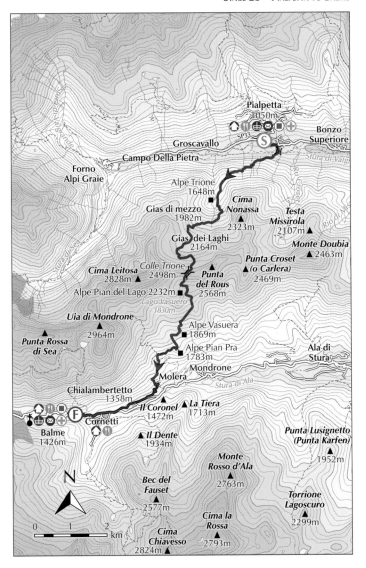

and the vegetation thins, becoming more alpine. A pretty waterfall cascades from the prominent Cima Nonassa (2323m) on your left. Follow the way markings as the path turns west here and past the huts in a clearing at **Gias di mezzo** (1982m), then after a way, turn south again climbing to the impressive cirque that houses the Laghi di Trione. Pass the abandoned farm huts of **Gias dei Laghi** (2164m), and loop east to find the narrow gully that climbs to the *colle* between Punta del Rous (2568m) and the east ridge of Cima Leitosa (2828m). Take care across late-lying snow that invariably sits in the north-facing cirque below **Colle Trione** (2498m).

Descend steeply south-west from the *colle*, bypassing steep crags, then turn back east for the final stretch to **Lago Vasuero** and **Alpe Pian del Lago** (2232m). Pass left of the huts and take the vague path down through dense alder shrub, bearing right past the rocky outcrop of Truc Armentera (2152m). Keep south-west now to cross the Rio della Chiesa, then turn left and descend to **Alpe Pian Pra** (1783m). Shortly after, pick up the small road that heads south-west for a short way, then take the path south across the corner of the road and on down to join the road from **Molera** west into **Balme**.

Posta Tappa GTA
Les Montagnards

FACILITIES INFORMATION FOR STAGE 25

Accommodation

Posto Tappa GTA Les Montagnards, mixed rooms, wifi, Frazione Cornetti, 73 Balme, (TO), +39 0123 233073

Villa Teja B&B, mixed rooms, wifi, Frazione Cornetti, 71 Balme, (TO), +39 349 447 8557

Amenities

Meals and limited snacks available at *posto tappa*.

Restaurants, post office and groceries as well as a sports shop in Balme.

Transport

A once daily bus runs from Balme to Germagnano, where a train departs hourly for Turin airport.

STAGE 26
Balme to Usseglio

Start	Balme (1426m)
Finish	Usseglio (1277m)
Distance	11.5km
Ascent	1175m
Descent	1400m
Time	6hr 30min

A stunning stage of saw-tooth crags, swirling mists and spectacular views among 3000m peaks. Also one of steep climbs, narrow paths, fallen trees and challenging terrain, so care is required, particularly on the decent. This is an epic adventure that will exhaust and delight in equal measure.

Leave **Balme** through Cornetti on the road leading south towards the tiny hamlet of **Fre**. As the road ends, take the wooden bridge left across the Rio Paschiet, then bear right and follow it upstream, climbing steadily beyond

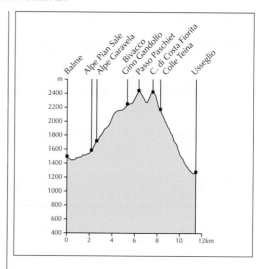

the huts at **Alpe Pian Sale** (1572m). Continue up the narrowing gorge past **Alpe Garavela** (1719m). At the head of this climb follow the path left below Alpe Pian Buet (2018m) to cross into the impressive cirque full of rock and scree, below Bec del Fauset (2579m). Then turn south once more to climb out of this to the tranquil, turquoise waters of **Laghi Verdi** (2156m). Continuing south, a short way further on you will find the neat little **Bivacco Gino Gandolfo** (2209m), diminutive among the gigantic slabs of grey stone above.

Bearing left now, on the west flank of Punta Golai (2818m), climb steadily over scree and rockfall, gradually gaining height, to reach **Passo Paschiet** (2431m), the first of three *colles* that must be crossed. The imposing northwest face of Torre d'Ovarda prevents a traverse directly south, so take the easy path ahead, keeping right at a path junction, and descend into a remote basin of pasture, dominated by an enormous rock that doubles as the back wall of a shepherd's hut. Here the headwaters of the Rio d'Ovarda provide refreshment, as well as stimulating a rich profusion of meadow wildflowers.

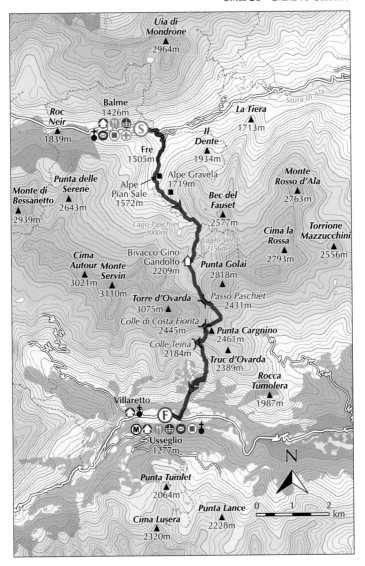

A careful look around this **pasture basin** reveals a wealth of small, simple engravings, probably done by shepherds over the centuries. These include a range of names, dates and Christian symbols.

Turn south-west once more to ascend the easy slope up to the **Colle di Costa Fiorita** (2445m), named for the wildflowers that are so prominent here. Leaving the ridge, keep left as the path traverses south above hazardous scree slopes, then bear right, descending a grassy ridge to the less obvious **Colle Teina** (2184m) where you gain first sight of the Valle di Viu, almost 1000m below. Begin the descent heading south-east from the *colle*, below crags to avoid the steepest section of slope. Turning south cross Pian Venaus, a pasture plateau, before descending further across the flank of the hill and over a tributary stream, through dense alpenrose shrub. Follow the path as it

The spires of Torre d'Ovarda Orientale

turns west now, descending steeply through a number of switchbacks, on a tricky section that requires concentration and careful foot placement. As you reach the *torrente* of Rio Venaus the gradient eases a little. Turn left and continue down the left bank of the *torrente* where occasional stone steps help with traction on the moss and slippery pine needles. As you descend right into the gully, join a stone retaining wall along the edge of the watercourse and follow this across a meadow into **Usseglio**.

FACILITIES INFORMATION FOR STAGE 26

Accommodation

Bivacco Gino Gandolfo, Presso Laghi Verdi, 10070 Balme (TO)

Posto Tappa GTA Albergo Furnasa, double and family rooms, wifi, Via XXIV Maggio, 16 Frazione Villaretto, Usseglio, (TO), +39 0123 83788

Albergo Rocciamelone, double and family rooms, wifi, Via Roma, 37 Usseglio, (TO), +39 0123 83743

Amenities

Meals and limited snacks available at accommodation providers.

Transport

Buses from Usseglio run four times a day to Germagnano, to connect with onward trains.

STAGE 27
Usseglio to Il Trucco

Start	Usseglio (1277m)
Finish	Il Trucco (1706m)
Distance	23km
Ascent	1430m
Descent	985m
Time	8hr 30min

A long stage, but with good way marking and paths, enabling swift progress, first to the panoramic views at the head of Valle di Viu, then a steady climb to the dramatic Colle of the Iron Cross, before dropping to cross the south face of Rocciamelone.

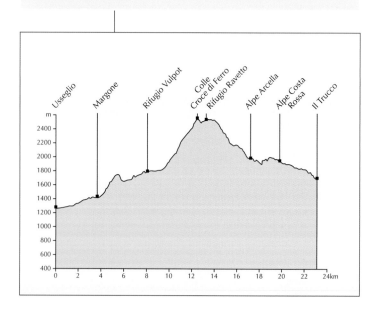

Leave **Usseglio** west on the quiet road to Margone. The route is tarmac for 3km, but it does not typically see a lot of traffic. As you enter **Margone**, pass the church and a broad car-parking area where an information board shows the GTA route to Lago di Malaciaussia. Take the small road left downhill to the *torrente* and across a bridge, then immediately right to follow the riverbank, past huts at **Vaiet** (1499m). Continue ahead climbing gently through shrub and trees, skirting left behind an elongated outcrop, then right back to the line of the *torrente*. Climbing more steeply now through a series of steps and across the *torrente*, arrive at promontory by a shrine, on a road bend, with views out across Lago di Malciaussia. Descend from here, a short distance to the **Rifugio Vulpot** (1805m).

Follow the track around the north side of the lake, ignore a side track and continue to cross the crumbling concrete bridge over the *torrente* that feeds the lake, then ignore a second side path and keep left to climb over a bluff. Only then turn south and climb more steeply. Keep right at a further track junction and make your way steadily up the gully of the Rio Croce di Ferro between scree slopes on your right and the cliffs of Monte Turlo (2590m) on your left. Bear left across the slope between crags for the final push to **Colle Croce di Ferro** (2546m). Ignoring a track on your left, descend across the *colle* then turn sharply right to contour around the slope, passing in front of the spectacularly located **Rifugio Capanna Sociale Aurelio Ravetto** (2545m).

Built as a military barracks between the two world wars, and situated on the slopes of Monte Palon (2965m) on the route of both the GTA and the Sentiero Italia, **Rifugio Capanna Sociale Aurelio Ravetto** was purchased by Mr Aurelio Ravetto and was privately owned until 2000, when it was gifted to a group of 12 members and manager, Franco Vigna, who formed the Association Social Hut Aurelio Ravetto to run and manage the hut.

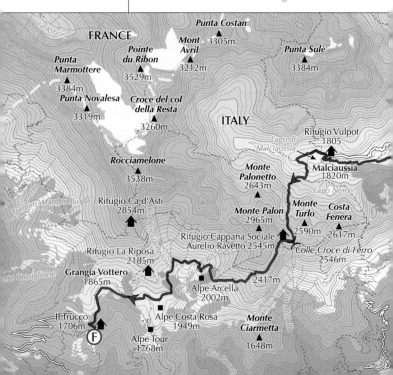

Continue south-west on a good, broadly level track above precipitous slopes, to bear right around the southern ridge of Monte Palon. Descending once more across steep pasture to cross the Cresta Creuse before descending to **Alpe Arcella** (2002m). From here a wonderful, gently descending gravel track can be taken, first contouring around the headwaters of the Torrente Rocciamelone, then west across the south flank of Rocciamelone (3538m) itself. Pass above **Alpe Costa Rossa** (1949m) and the turning for Alpe Tour, opposite a track junction leading to Rifugio La Riposa (2185m). A short way beyond, as you enter trees, leave the track on the left and head downhill. At **Grangia Vottero** (1865m), don't go through the farm to the track, but keep left descending around the hill to reach a lower track that leads you to the cluster of dwellings that make up **Il Trucco** (1706m).

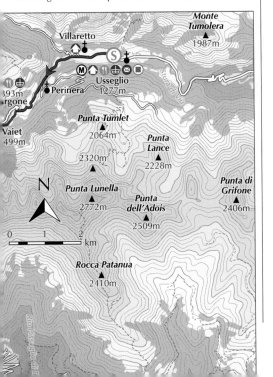

ROCCIAMELONE

At the southern end of the Graian Alps, standing conical above its surroundings at 3,538m, Rocciamelone (meaning crumbly rock) was for centuries believed to be the highest mountain in the Alps. Clearly visible from the ancient Roman city of Susa on the plain, the peak is perhaps one of the most visited peaks in the Alps, due both to the ease of access and the traditional annual pilgrimage on August 5. It was first climbed on 1st September 1358 by Bonifacius Rotarius (of Asti) who, according to legend, erected a small metal likeness of the Virgin Mary in gratitude for surviving captivity in the Holy Land during a war against the Muslims. Later in 1899 this was replaced with a huge, three-metre high, 650kg statue, and it has become a key religious pilgrimage site since. An excursion to the summit is worth the extra time and a detour can be made by taking path 530 after the Colle della Croce di Ferro to stay at the Rifugio Cà d'Asti (2854m) on the slopes below the summit, enabling a sunrise summit before descending to Il Trucco.

FACILITIES INFORMATION FOR STAGE 27

Accommodation

Rifugio Vulpot, dormitory, mixed rooms, wifi, Frazione Malciaussia, Usseglio, (TO), +39 0123 83771

Rifugio Capanna Sociale Aurelio Ravetto, mixed rooms, Colle della Crocedi Ferro, Bussoleno, (TO), +39 338 900 7813

Rifugio La Riposa, dormitory, Alpe la Riposa, Mompantero, (TO), +39 0122 675173

Rifugio Il Truc, mixed rooms, Borgata Trucco, Mompantero, (TO), +39 0122 32963, +39 349 805 3424

Rifugio Cà d'Asti, dormitory, 10059 Mompantero, (TO), +39 0122 33192

Amenities

Meals and limited snacks available at accommodation providers.

Transport

None on route.

STAGE 28
Il Trucco to Susa

Start	Il Trucco (1706m)
Finish	Susa (494m)
Distance	7km
Ascent	5m
Descent	1210m
Time	2hr 45min

A short stage into Susa allows time for transport arrangements, or indeed an early hotel check in to enable laundry and shopping. Nonetheless, it's not to be rushed. An evocative descent with extensive views across the bustling plain below encourages reflection on the journey. Susa itself, an ancient Roman city, has much to offer too and a few extra hours here provide a welcome chance to explore.

Leave **Il Trucco** following the well-marked path south-west between summer huts, from the track bear left to a path leading to a viewpoint at the brow of the hill at **Casa Praletto**. This is where the real descent begins. A little further down the path touches on the end of a gravel track. Bear left here and continue downhill more steeply. This section was burned a few years ago and has been slow to show signs of recovery. While any tree markings are gone, some blazes on stones remain and are a useful guide to keep you on track as the path switches back and forth, passing old huts at **Casa Molinetto** (1349m) and **Casa Pian Berca** a short way further on. At Ponte Pietrabruna cross the road and descend straight ahead into trees. After a short distance the path bears left and you

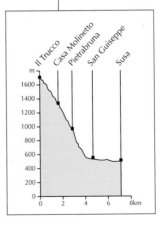

will emerge on a track alongside a shrine at **Pietrabruna** itself (1052m). Keep ahead past a second shrine at **Castagneretto** (943m) then cross a small track. The final stage of the descent is steeper, dry and scrubby, but the views across the valley make up for this.

The path narrows to a squeeze behind small old houses that have been built about as far back into the hillside as possible, then suddenly drops out onto a road junction at the base of the hill in **San Guiseppe** (555m). Here signposting suggests going straight across the junction and over the river. This is an unpleasant route that would have you negotiate the edge of a busy slip road to

Rocciamelone from the Convento Hotel in Susa

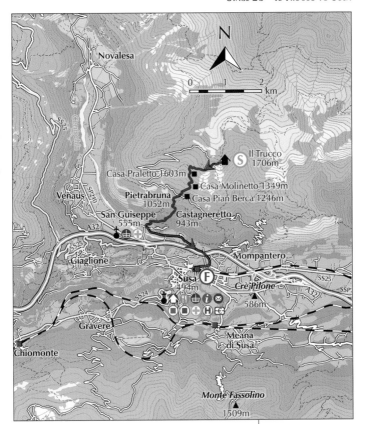

the toll road thundering above. Follow the original GTA route left at the junction and along the quiet road north of the river, through the hamlets of Marzano and Trinita, then follow the road round to the right into the north edge of **Susa**, where you reach a junction by a bridge over the river. Turn right and cross the bridge continuing straight ahead to pass behind Susa railway station. If you are staying at the Hotel Susa & Stazione turn left here and walk to the end of the road where it is ahead.

FACILITIES INFORMATION FOR STAGE 28

Accommodation

Hotel Susa & Stazione, double and triple rooms, wifi, laundry, Corso Stati Uniti 4 / 6, 10059 SUSA (TO), +39 0 122 622 226

Centro Beato Rosaz Monastery, double and family rooms, wifi, Via Madonna Delle Grazie, 4 Susa, (TO), +39 0122 622461

Convento Boutique hotel, double and family rooms, wifi, Piazza San Francesco 5, 10059 Susa (TO), T +39 0122 622548

L'Archivolto B&B, double and family rooms, wifi, Vicolo Gran Valentino, 12 Susa (TO), T +39 349 670 5887

Amenities

Meals and limited snacks available at some accommodation providers.

Plenty of options for restaurants, groceries, post office, laundry and so on in Susa.

Transport

Susa is connected to Turin by railway and the journey takes around 1hr, with regular buses to Turin airport adding another 50min and departing every 20min from the city centre. To connect to Milan Malpensa airport from Turin bus or train can be taken, with each taking around a further 2hr.

STAGE 29

Susa to Alpe Toglie

Start	Susa (494m)
Finish	Alpe Toglie (1564m)
Distance	11.75km
Ascent	1140m
Descent	85m
Time	5hr

Despite leaving through the suburbs of the town, this is a surprisingly interesting and varied stage with much to see en route. From historic hamlets and cobbled streets, to orchards, woods and vineyards, this is a pleasant and never too strenuous walk.

From the bridge over the river at the centre of **Susa** head south, on Via Norberto Rosa, climbing through the historic 'old quarter' of the town to a major road junction.

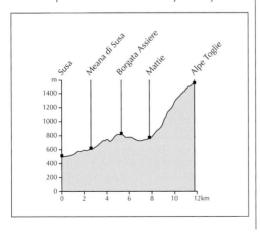

Cross this and take the small road left through a residential street. Red/white blazes on posts keep you on track through a couple of corners before the path narrows to a gravel track, walled on one side as you head out past fields then into trees, before joining a road end into **Meana di Susa** (587m). At the T-junction turn left and pass the railway station, then at the end of the road turn right, passing under the railway bridge and follow the road around to the left, uphill. After a short distance take a signposted path sharply left to climb to a residential street end. Proceed ahead, over a junction, then at the corner ahead on another small path to the next road. Cross and keep left at the fork then left again at a junction aside a shrine into Via Suffis.

Follow this for some way now, as it narrows through houses, then widens again, before switchbacks enable

The path out of Susa

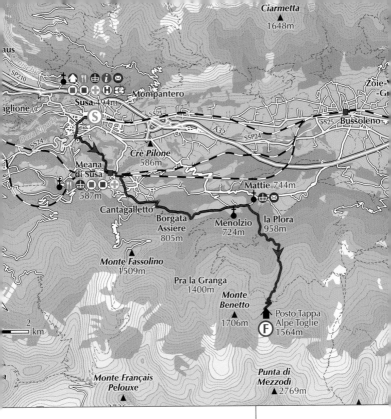

the climb up the hillside on your right. A path cuts the
corner on the second bend, then continue ahead through
the hamlet of **Borgata Assiere** (805m) and beyond on a
simple track past woods and orchards, eventually entering the settlement of **Menolzio** (724m). Ascend gently
along the narrow street, past water fountains, between
old houses, then across the river where a GTA sign confirms the route. A short way further on take a signposted
right turn on a gravel track uphill to a picnic area. Turn
right again here uphill until the road turns right across
the *torrente*. Just before this, take a path left off the road,
signposted Alpe Toglie. After 15min cross a clearing and
rise to the unpaved road leading to **Alpe Toglie**.

FACILITIES INFORMATION FOR STAGE 29

Accommodation
Posto Tappa Alpe Toglie, dormitory, Localita Toglie, Mattie, (TO), +39 366 444 8964

Amenities
Meals available at accommodation provider.

Transport
Local rail and bus connections at Meana di Susa.

STAGE 30
Alpe Toglie to Usseaux

Start	Alpe Toglie (1564m)
Finish	Usseaux (1404m)
Distance	15.5km
Ascent	1245m
Descent	1355m
Time	6hr 45min

A steady climb to Colle dell'Orsiera is rewarded with views and historic fortifications. The best of the stage is the latter however with wooded hillside, ancient villages, more fortifications and floral displays both wild and cultivated. A side trip to the upper fort of Fenestrelle is an easy detour and the historic Hotel Pracatinat nearby, high on the hillside, enables an early finish for those wishing to take their time.

Returning to the head of the track, turn left and continue past the cow shed, then right, keeping right again at a subsequent track fork. Climb north-west through dense trees to crest the ridge at **Monte Benetto** (1706m), ignore a side track, turn immediately south and continue up

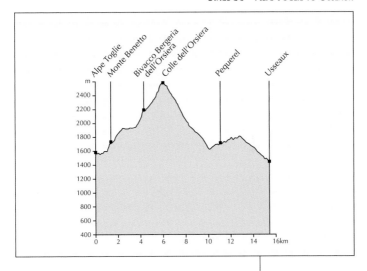

the ridge to a spur marked as Monte Genta (1883m), then follow the well-marked path south-west to reach **Bivacco Bergeria dell'Orsiera** (1931m). Ignore the side path here and continue south-west. The going becomes tougher through dense alder but the *colle* is visible ahead in the saddle between Monte Orsiera and Roc Ciardonet. Beyond the thicket follow the path up short, steep and eroded switchbacks in the final ascent to **Colle dell'Orsiera** (2595m).

> The defensive stone wall across the saddle at **Colle dell'Orsiera** dates from the mid-eighteenth century as part of fortifications built to protect against French invasion.

Descend south-west around the flank of Roc Ciardonet. As the path steepens keep right at a path junction. A pleasant enough descent ensues, from scree to pasture and then into trees. Cross a small road and shortly after bear right down the hill into the tiny village of **Puy**. Follow the path around the slope and slightly

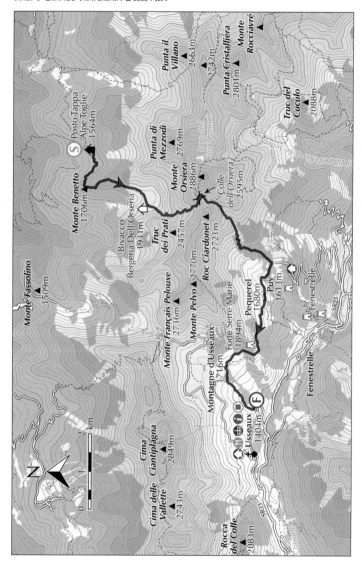

The great fortress of Fenestrelle

uphill through, only slightly larger, **Pequerel** (1680m). As you exit the village ignore the first path downhill and follow the road to the top of the corner to take the second path ascending slightly, broadly west.

> As you leave **Pequerel**, glance back at the top of the village and notice the impressive stone-built avalanche defences that date back to 1716.

The narrow path from Pequerel is easily followed despite the verdant growth and abundant wildflowers. Keep west until several clearings enable good views directly up the slope to the imposing **Forte Serre Marie** (1894m), then follow the contour north before gradually descending around the headwaters of the Rio d'Usseaux. The path leads into the top of the wonderfully floral **Usseaux** (1404m). ▶

> **Usseaux** is heralded as one of the most beautiful villages in all of Italy, having won awards for its floral displays and murals depicting mountain village

Those keen to take a closer look at the Fenestrelle fortifications could drop down the road from Puy to Forte delle Valli. A short footpath from there leads to the intriguing 1930s Hotel Pracatinat.

life, animals, even fairy tales. It's cobbled streets and traditional architecture are a joy to explore and visitors are encouraged to allow a little extra time to do so.

FACILITIES INFORMATION FOR STAGE 30

Accommodation
Bivacco Bergeria dell'Orsiera, dormitory, Bergeria dell'Orsiera, Mattie, (TO), +39 0122 47064

Hotel Pracatinat, double and family rooms, wifi, Località Prà Catinat, 2, 10060 Fenestrelle (TO), +39 0121 884884

La Placette di Elisa Blanc, double and triple rooms, Via della chiesa 5, 10060 Usseaux, (TO), +39 0121 83073, +39 349 370 1722

Hotel Lago Laux, double and triple rooms, Via al Lago, 7 Localita Lago Laux, Usseaux, (TO), +39 0121 83944

Amenities
Meals and limited snacks available at accommodation providers.

Simple restaurant and ATM in Usseaux.

Transport
Bus stop is on the main road below Usseaux. Buses leave three times a day for the 10min ride to Fenestrelle. From there connecting buses can be taken to onward destinations.

STAGE 31

Usseaux to Balsiglia

Start	Usseaux (1404m)
Finish	Balsiglia (1387m)
Distance	19km
Ascent	1360m
Descent	1430m
Time	7hr 45min

An easy start with the picturesque hamlet of Laux worth a detour, but not for long as this is a long stage, but scenic, with a remote feel crossing one of the higher passes on the route where late snow can linger amid the abandoned forts. A long descent along the Germansca torrente follows, into the historic battleground of Balsiglia where, with prior arrangement, accommodation providers from further down the road will collect weary trekkers.

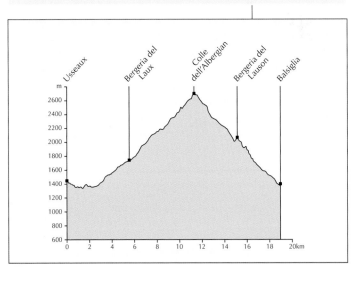

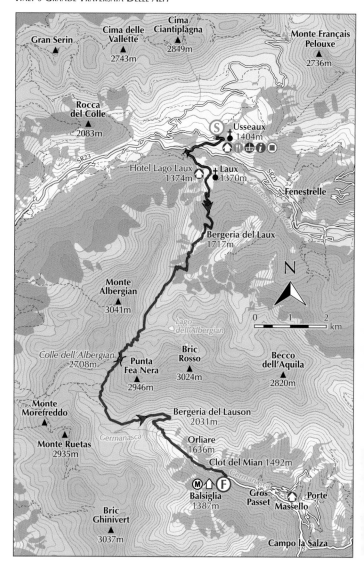

Head down the road from **Usseaux** to the junction, turn right then left to descend the small road towards Laux, crossing the Torrente Chisone. A short way further, on your right pass the beautiful location of the **Hotel Lago Laux** and continue up the road to the hamlet of **Laux**.

> The trail only touches on the upper edge of the hamlet of **Laux**, but it is a beautiful place that is well worth taking the time for a walk through and explore.

From the road end at Laux take the good track sign-posted right, climbing broadly south, through pasture then up into the woods, through a series of switchbacks as the gradient increases. At a clearing, pass the huts at **Bergeria del Laux** (1717m) and keep right at a fork, then continue into further woodland amid the mysterious carvings that add an element of fairytale to the woods. At a track junction ignore the left to Bergeria del Pra and turn right, ascending steeply uphill on a series of short switchbacks. A long stretch of gentle climb above the Rio dell'Albergian now ensues on a good path through

Former military barracks occupies a coveted position

grazed pasture. Above to your right towers Monte Albergian (3041m) with plenty of evidence around of the gradual erosion that results in the scattered boulders that dot the hillside. As you climb make increasing use of the switchbacks that ease the gradient. A glance back to the left reveals the remains of a military barracks on the far side of the *torrente*, and behind, almost hidden from view, the Lago dell'Albergian.

The final section to the pass becomes steeper, rocky and dramatic. At the **Colle dell'Albergian** (2708m) the view opens up to reveal the Barre des Ecrins ahead. Between the Monte Grand Miuls (2971m) on your right and Punta Fea Nera (2946m) on your left, the *colle* is a strategic viewpoint and it is easy to see why the presence of military posts is so great.

The descent is a straightforward affair. Ignore the side track and cross the *colle* straight ahead. Following a short section of scree and a brief series of switchbacks,

WALDESIAN PERSECUTION AND RESISTANCE

The small museum at Balsiglia is worth visiting if you have any interest at all in the history of the Waldesian persecution and resistance. From the 12th century to the 17th, the Waldensian people were persecuted and suffered terribly following declaration of their 'heresy' by the Catholic Church. In January 1686 the Duke of Savoy had followed the French lead in again removing protections for protestants in Piedmont and a further period of persecution ensued. At the tail end of a significant resistance in the winter of 1689, with the support of protestant reformers from northern Europe, in particular the Dutch under William of Orange, just 360 Waldensians remained, defending the stronghold of Balsiglia against some 4000 French troops. The final French assault was delayed by storm and cloud. The French commander was so confident of victory that he sent word to Paris of success. However, when the French awoke the next morning, they found the valleys empty. The Waldensians under the cover of cloud and darkness had descended from the peak and escaped. Just a few days later, a change in political alliances led to a grant of religious freedoms and ended the persecution.

Access to the museum can be arranged through Pierluigi Bertalotto of Agriturismo La Miando.

descend to a wonderful grass plateau housing further military ruins. Beyond this another steeper section leads to a further shelf of pasture, now above the gully of the Germansca di Massello, with the pyramid of Monte Ruetas (2935m) towering behind. Descending into this, keep left and follow the sporadically marked path to a signed track junction then turn left. Keep left now in an arc around the base of a scree slope and down into the gully of a small tributary, before a more level traverse east, towards the huts of **Bergeria del Lauson** (2031m). A short way before the huts, follow the path right in descent in an almost 180-degree turn back along the slope to the confluence of tributaries, then turn left, heading south-east now, for the final stretch descending parallel to the *torrente* all the way to Balsiglia. At the foot of the steeper section of descent is the most advantageous view of the Cascata del Pis waterfall on your right. Descend into **Balsiglia** between buildings and descend to the car park. ▶

The posto tappa at Balsiglia is a self-catering hut (no shop). Arrangements can be made in advance with La Foresteria or La Miando for pick-up from Balsiglia, saving 2/4km road walk.

FACILITIES INFORMATION FOR STAGE 31

Accommodation

La Foresteria di Massello, double and family rooms, wifi, Via Molino, 4 Frazione Molino, Massello, (TO), +39 0121 808678, +39 366 818 3564

Agriturismo La Miando, double rooms, wifi, Baita Didiero, 16 Salza di Pinerolo, (TO), +39 0121 188 0034, +39 339 276 3215

The *posto tappa* at Balsiglia is on the top floor of the old museum and is a self-catering hut. There is no shop in Balsiglia so you must carry supplies for dinner if you plan to stay there. Alternatively, arrangements can be made in advance with the hosts at either La Foresteria or La Miando for pick-up from Balsiglia, saving 2/4km road walk.

Amenities

Meals and limited snacks available at accommodation providers.

Transport

None on route.

STAGE 32

Balsiglia to Ghigo di Prali

Start	Balsiglia (1387m)
Finish	Ghigo di Prali (1451m)
Distance	16km
Ascent	845m
Descent	765m
Time	6hr 15min

Depending on your accommodation choices this stage may be up to 4km shorter if you took the option of a pick-up to overnight at Massello or Didiero. If not then the stage commences with a road section downhill through forest. Moderate climbs to two *colles* are separated by the lovely hamlet of Roderetto before a short descent into Ghigo di Prali.

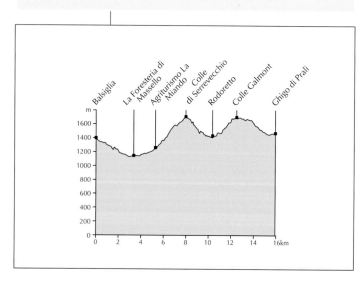

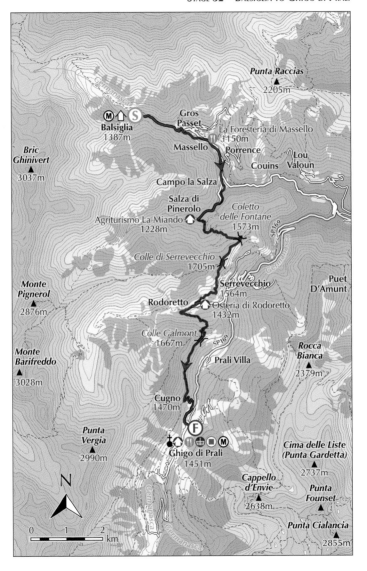

From **Balsiglia** take the road south-east passing through
the hamlets of **Gros Passet** and Piccolo Passet (1226m),
just beyond which there is an option to cross the *torrente* on a footpath to re-join the road after a short way.
Little is to be gained by this other than a break from the
monotony of the road. Continuing down the hill, pass
through the collection of hamlets that together are known
as **Massello**, and on the right **La Foresteria di Massello**
(1150m). Keep right as the road forks, signposted Didiero.
Shortly after, on a side road between houses, drop to the
torrente before rising and re-joining the road once more.
Eventually the main road ends in the hamlet of Didiero.
On the right is **Agriturismo La Miando** (1228m).

Continue over a bridge across the *torrente* to find a
sign board marked GTA. Turn left here and ascend the
gravel track. The path cuts directly across a succession of
switchbacks, climbing directly to **Colletto delle Fontane**
(1573m). Turn right and follow the ridge south-west to
reach **Colle di Serrevecchio** (1705m). From here descend
gradually south through the hamlet of **Serrevecchio**
(1564m) to reach **Rodoretto** and the **Osteria di Rodoretto**

(1432m). Bear right between houses out of Rodoretto, as far as the road hairpin. Here, take the gravel track ahead, down to the stream. Cross, turn left and ascend south-east cutting across track switchbacks on a small path if the vegetation has been cut. Bear right across the ridge at **Colle Galmont** (1667m) then traverse the slope for a way before joining a mountain bike track to descend left, past the couple of houses at **Cugno** (1470m). Join the main road, but instead of turning right, turn left then drop to the river before then turning right to follow the *torrente* for a short way into **Ghigo di Prali**. This is more pleasant than the road, and a small path enables you to step up to the road at the bridge. The Albergo delle Alpi is straight ahead on the right.

FACILITIES INFORMATION FOR STAGE 32

Accommodation

Osteria di Rodoretto, double rooms, Baita Rodoretto, 19 Prali, (TO), +39 389 296 9845

Albergo delle Alpi, double and family rooms, wifi, Frazione Ghigo, 10 Prali, (TO), +39 0121 807537

Casa Alpa Ca B&B, double rooms, wifi, Borgata Orgere, 20 Prali, (TO), +39 333 794 4935

Amenities

Meals and limited snacks available at accommodation providers.

A number of restaurants and bars in the centre of Ghigo and a mini-market and sports shop further up the road.

Transport

Bus 303 leaves Ghigo four times a day to Perosa Argentina (45min) where connecting buses can be taken via Pinerolo to Turin.

STAGE 33
Ghigo di Prali to Villanova

Start	Ghigo di Prali (1451m)
Finish	Villanova (1231m)
Distance	19km
Ascent	1210m
Descent	1425m
Time	8hr

There are two options at the outset of this stage, the footpath, or the chairlift that lifts the hiker to the Tredici Laghi (the thirteen lakes). The chairlift is a wonderful option to enable views of Monte Rosa and an impeccable military track traverses to the Colle Giullian for a spectacular view of Monviso. The descent is less scenic, but made easy by vehicle track servicing the *alpe* farm at Bergerie Giulian.

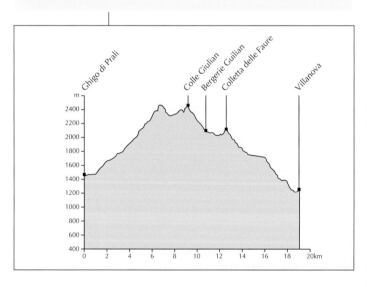

Leaving **Ghigo di Prali**, head south-west, up the valley towards **Malzat**, past the ski rentals and the chairlift station. Continue up the road to the parking area where the tarmac road ends. Take the track that continues beyond, and after a short distance take the side track left signposted Agriturismo Miandette. Follow this uphill, through a steep switchback, then left again to join an upper track. Turn right here and follow the track to a signposted path, climbing left around the south-facing flank of the hill. At a track junction below the lakes and military ruins, keep right and take the old military road that leads, at times steeply, over the north-west ridge of Punta Cornourin (2701m), dropping into the gully beyond, then subsequently over the north-west ridge of Monte Peigro (2665m), to reach **Colle Giulian** (2451m).

The **chairlift** rises in two stages changing at Pian Alpet. From the upper station at Bric Rond (2477m), take the path south-east to the lakes. Turn right at the initial track junction, dropping south-west, then left to re-join the main route on the traverse to Colle Giulian. Note that some guides and maps (including

Military road between the colle and the Tredici Laghi

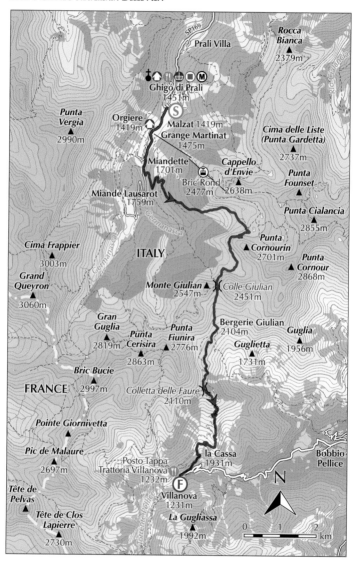

Nat Geo mapping) show a footpath directly from the chairlift station to the Tredici Laghi track. In the summer this is a mountain bike descent, with signs strictly forbidding hikers. If not taking the chairlift, continue up the road as outlined above.

Cross the *colle* heading south after a couple of short switchbacks, fairly directly down to **Bergerie Guilian** (2104m), once abandoned, now a working summer farm. Keep right and follow the *alpe* track from here across welcome level ground. After a couple of stream crossings bear right uphill to reach the **Colletta delle Faure** (2110m). Re-joining the *alpe* track descend left steeply downhill. Keeping to the nose of the ridge the path begins cut across the switchbacks as they grow wider. Eventually leave the track and continue down the ridgeline to meet a lower track at Culubrusa (1446m). Follow this across the slope and over the *torrente*, then leave it and descend to another track corner. Take the lower track left downhill and into **Villanova**.

FACILITIES INFORMATION FOR STAGE 33

Accommodation
Posto Tappa Trattoria Villanova, dormitory and basic rooms, Via Villanova, 1 Bobbio Pellice, (TO), +39 0121 957850

Amenities
Meals and limited snacks available at accommodation providers.

Transport
None on route.

STAGE 34
Villanova to Rifugio Barbara Lowrie

Start	Villanova (1231m)
Finish	Rifugio Barbara Lowrie (1753m)
Distance	12.5km
Ascent	1175m
Descent	655m
Time	5hr 45min

A steady climb alongside the *torrente*, past waterfalls and barely visible historic military ruins for an early opportunity for refreshment at the fabulous Rifugio Willy Jervis. From there the climb to Rifugio Barant is steeper but rewarding and the alpine botanical garden is not to be missed. Much of the descent is on good tracks accompanied by the ever-present marmots.

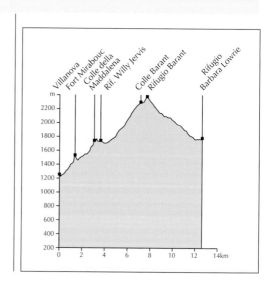

Leave **Villanova** heading south-west, passing **Case Brunel** (1306m) and continuing to join a track at the site of the former **Fort Mirabouc**.

From Rifugio Willy Jervis: view to the head of Valle Pellice

> While little remains of **Fort Mirabouc** today, it was once a significant fortification, built between 1565 and 1569 by the Duke of Savoy and used as part of efforts to contain and suppress the Waldensians and their proto-protestant ideology. Having changed hands between French and Ducal forces several times, the French eventually blew the fort up in 1794.

Turn left and head south here, past the waterfall (another Cascata del Pis) on your right, and continue above the Torrente Pellice, shortcutting track corners a couple of times, then leaving the track before it crosses the *torrente*, to take the path over the diminutive rise of **Colle della Maddalena** (1742m). The tiny community of Ciabot del Pra and the prominent **Rifugio Willy Jervis** (1732m) are now ahead of you. If you are continuing,

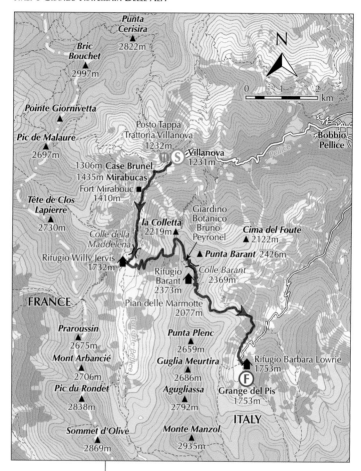

turn left in front of the *rifugio* and descend to the vehicle track. Turn left to cross the *torrente*, then bear right initially uphill before continuing up through woods across switchbacks to lessen the gradient. As you gain height the tree cover thins and after a long push, bear right, across the west flank of Punta Barant (2425m).

At the Colle Barant, some 2369m above sea level, sits the **Bruno Peyronel Alpine Botanical Garden**. The garden is located within the wider Prà-Barant Wildlife Oasis which was established in 1976 by ministerial decree from the Province of Turin, on the territory of a former municipal hunting reserve. Classified as a Site of Community Interest for its remarkable botanical and faunal merits, it has a total area of approximately 4,000 hectares, equal to 13% of the area of the entire valley. It is bounded by the upper course of the Pellice stream to the northwest, the entire course of the Guicchard stream to the east, and with the Queyras Natural Park in France, and the Po Cuneese Park to the south.

The garden, named after Bruno Peyronel, a well-known naturalist and botanist originally from the Valdesi valleys, was opened in 1991 with the aim of studying and protecting the unique flora. In this area of just over one hectare, multiple natural environments can be found including rock, various types of pasture, wetlands, and shrubs. The Alpine Botanical Association has identified more than 300 different species of alpine flora, of which more than thirty are endemic. Ibex and wolves have also now repopulated the area, underlining its importance as a protected area,

Just below the *colle* sits the **Rifugio Barant** (2373m), recently refurbished and reopened. The descent from here is steep and a series of long switchbacks make this easier, although a path does cut across them directly. Follow the track down, past a shrine at **Pian delle Marmotte** (2077m), and on, crossing several tributary streams. Continue bearing right as the track skirts below a promontory in gradual descent. Ignore the first small side track to your right, continue to join the larger road up from the valley at a parking area and information board. Turn right here to continue up the road to **Rifugio Barbara Lowrie** (1753m).

FACILITIES INFORMATION FOR STAGE 34

Accomodation

Rifugio Willy Jervis, dormitory and mixed rooms, Ciabot del Pra', Bobbio Pellice (TO), +39 0121 932755, +39 0121 197 6249

Rifugio Barant, dormitory, Colle del Baracun, Bobbio Pellice (TO), +39 0121 197 6278, +39 335 627 6850

Rifugio Barbara Lowrie, mixed rooms, Frazione Grange del Pis, Bobbio Pellice, (TO), +39 0121 930077

Amenities

Meals and limited snacks available at accommodation providers.

Transport

None on route.

STAGE 35

Rifugio Barbara Lowrie to Rifugio Quintino Sella

Start	Rifugio Barbara Lowrie (1753m)
Finish	Rifugio Quintino Sella (2640m)
Distance	14km
Ascent	1440m
Descent	560m
Time	6hr 30min

A truly rewarding climb through conifer-clad hillside, with successive copses rich in fern, alpenrose and wildflower, and dotted with boulders. Clear tracks make easy going to Pian del Re where refreshment from the source of the Po is most welcome, before climbing again through the rock and scree of the upper mountain environment, to the foot of Monviso itself.

The biodiverse slopes of Rocca Bianca

Leave **Rifugio Barbara Lowrie** and head south across the meadow behind the hut. This is grazed by cattle and unclear in places, but head for the narrowing between the stream and the trees at the base of the slope. At the narrow section turn left and take the small signposted path steeply uphill south-east. This is a beautiful stage through mossy boulders, heather and verdant growth, also home to a rare, endemic black salamander. The undergrowth is thinning by **Colle Proussera** (2182m), but the climb continues. Follow the path on up the ridgeline, but as it steepens keep left to traverse the east face of Rocca Nera (2717m). Cross the lower scree slopes then climb to cross the ridge at **Colle della Gianna** (2531m).

Bear right around the ridge and traverse the slope south-west, then south, rising again just a little to the pass at **La Sellaccia** (2367m). A brief side-trip left is worthwhile here to the point of Truc Battaglie (2372m),

197

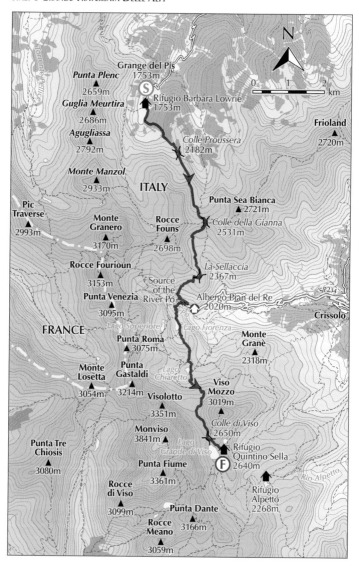

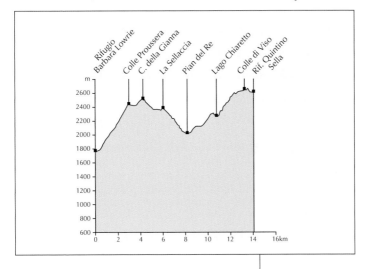

just to appreciate the layout of the valley below, and the giants ahead. Descend south-west, keeping right at the fork, through successive switchbacks to reach **Pian del Re** (2020m) and the eponymous *albergo*. Turning right here, continue to the road end and a clear, marked footpath can be taken left, across the source of the Po River before climbing to, and around the left side of **Lago Fiorenza**. Keep left at the fork and continue south, rising to the Colletto su Vallone dei Quarti (2260m). Shortly after at a track junction, turn left and descend a short way to cross the plain on the left side of **Lago Chiaretto** (2276m). Climb the scrubby slope on the far side to join the larger track and keep left again.

Climb again bearing broadly right through switch-backs that ease the gradient effectively. With Monviso's main summit of Punta Trieste (3841m) now towering above on your right and the pyramid of Viso Mozzo (3019m) dominating the skyline on your left, climb through the saddle in between, keeping to the left side and rising to the **Colle di Viso** (2650m) at the far end. As you do, the view of **Lago Grande di Viso** opens ahead. Take the clear path south-east now to the **Rifugio Quintino Sella** (2640m), the highest manned hut on the route.

MONVISO

Second in height only to Monte Rosa in the Piedmont, and with a pyramid shape towering some 500m above its immediate peers, Monviso (or Monte Viso) is easily identifiable from a considerable distance. It is said to be visible from as far as Mont Blanc and, on a clear day, even Milan Cathedral. The area surrounding Monviso was declared a cross-border UNESCO biosphere reserve in 2013, and the northern slopes feed the headwaters of the Po, Italy's longest river. It was climbed for the first time in modern history on August 30, 1861 by a team led by William Matthews (1828–1901), an English mountaineer, botanist and surveyor, also famed for proposing the formation of the Alpine Club of London in 1857. The cultural history of the mountain goes back much further, however. In ancient times it was known by the name Vesulus and was referenced in works by literary figures such as Chaucer and Dante. Further back, as far as 5000BC, the mountain was the site of a neolithic jadeite quarry. At an elevation of around 2000–2400m, the extracted stone was used to make ceremonial axe heads which have been found as far away as Western Ireland.

The Monviso massif carries another title, too however, one often missed by visitors; that of having one of the oldest mountain tunnels in Italy, possibly even the most ancient in Europe. Excavated during the Renaissance in 1479, it is located about 8km north of the main summit. The tunnel is 75m long, 3m wide and at an altitude of 2822m, links the villages of Crissolo, in the province of Cuneo on the Italian side, with Ristolas in the French department of Hautes-Alpes. Built for the purpose of trade, the tunnel made the crossing of the alpine barrier much easier for merchant caravans, and increased the number of days that trade was possible before winter snows closed trade routes. After about 120 years as a valuable route for both trade and military crossings, the Treaty of Lyon in 1601 saw political changes that led to the closure of the tunnel in favour of other routes. After sporadic openings, and subsequent closure due to rockfall several times over the centuries, the tunnel was reopened in 1907 thanks to the work of the Italian Alpine Club and government funding. Now under the auspices of the Rotary Club of Saluzzo, the tunnel has become an established link within the network of mountain paths in the Monviso region, as an alternative to crossing the summit of the Col de la Traversette.

FACILITIES INFORMATION FOR STAGE 35

Accommodation
Albergo Pian del Re, mixed rooms, Pian del Re, Crissolo, (CN), +39 0175 94967

Rifugio Pian della Regina, dormitory and mixed rooms, Localita Pian della Regina, 34 Crissolo, (CN), +39 0175 94907

Rifugio Qunitino Sella, mixed rooms, Lago Grande di Viso, Crissolo, (CN), +39 0175 994943

Rifugio Alpetto, mixed rooms, Lago di Alpetto, Oncino, (CN), +39 0175 576113, +39 340 513 0792

Amenities
Meals and limited snacks available at accommodation providers.

Transport
None on route.

STAGE 36
Rifugio Quintino Sella to Castello

Start	Rifugio Quintino Sella (2640m)
Finish	Castello (1590m)
Distance	11km
Ascent	190m
Descent	1240m
Time	4hr

A simple stage, walked almost entirely in descent, rounding the southern end of the Monviso massif through a moonscape of moraine and rockfall. Crossing patches of late-lying snow is likely until you reach the lower tree-clad slopes and easier walking alongside the Torrente Vallanta, leading to the Lago di Castello.

Beneath the east flank of Monviso, likely glowing orange as it catches the morning sun, turn south and head out along the path above the lake, keeping an eye on the

Monviso at dawn

ridges above where ibex regularly roam. Ignore the side tracks that lead right to the Passo delle Sagnette (2990m), the gateway to the summits above, and keep right at the fork (the left being the route to Rifugio Alpetto below).

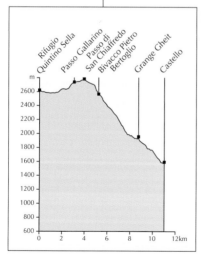

Passing to the right of **Lago delle Sagnette**, continue to traverse below the slope, eventually rising to the right to cross the **Passo Gallarino** (2728m) where the path divides. Take the right fork and cross the slope above both the Piano Gallarino and Lago, keeping just a couple of hundred metres below the summit of Punta Trento (2967m) to reach the **Passo di San Chiaffredo** (2764m).

Below the crest, cross a plateau of lakes, passing three to reach a side track signposting Bivacco Pietro Bertoglio (2770m) just ten minutes from the main route. The signpost confirms this as about midway, so continue south-west towards Grange Gheit, dropping more steeply now alongside a *torrente* into the Vallone delle Giargiatte. Continue past a side track on the right and, as the rock gradually gives way to conifer, descend through the Bosco dell'Alevè forest. The path bears left initially, ignore another side track here, then bear right as the gradient lessens to emerge from the trees at a small wooden crossing of the Torrente Vallanta at Grange Gheit (1930m).

The **Bosco dell'Alevè** (the name being derived from the old Occitan language) is considered an ancient or original woodland of around 90 per cent pine

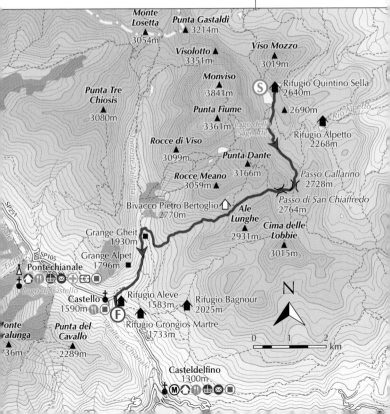

trees with about 10 per cent being larch. Covering as much as 825 hectares across the municipalities of Casteldelfino, Pontechianale and Sampeyre, it is the southernmost ancient forest in Europe and therefore an important protected area. Recorded since Roman times, the woods of Alevè contain many ancient trees. The oldest cembro pines in the forest (now a rare species, once commonplace) are over 500 years old.

Now cross the *torrente* to the broad track, turn left and follow an undulating path, keeping the *torrente* on your left, eventually arriving at a trailhead and information board alongside the main road. Turn right here to descend into **Castello** (or indeed beyond the lake, to Pontechianale), or left across the *torrente* and descend the road a short way to the **Rifugio Alevè**.

FACILITIES INFORMATION FOR STAGE 36

Accommodation
Bivacco Pietro Bertoglio, dormitory, Vallone delle Giargiatte, Lago del Prete, Pontechianale, (CN), +39 0175 33472

Rifugio Alevè, double and mixed rooms, wifi, Frazione Castello, 60 Pontechianale, (CN), +39 347 767 2234

Rifugio Grongios Martre, mixed rooms, wifi, Frazione Villaretto, Pontechianale, (CN), +39 340 069 2705

Rifugio Bagnour, mixed rooms, Valle Varaita, 12020 Maddalena, (CN), +39 320 426 0190

Amenities
Meals and limited snacks available at accommodation providers.

Restaurant in Castello. Further facilities including groceries in Pontechianale at the other end of the lake, or around 4km SE down the road in Casteldelfino.

Transport
From Castello the bus to Saluzzo runs three times a day taking about 1hr 15min. Connections from Saluzzo include bus to Turin, taking about 1hr 20min, with Milan a further 50min by train.

SECTION 3:
GTA South – Castello to Ventimiglia

Tranquility at Lago di Malinvern (Stage 43)

SECTION 3:
GTA South – Castello to Ventimiglia

Distance	283.5km
Ascent	17,780m
Descent	19,395m
Maps	IGC Nos 6, 7, 8 & 14, 1/50k; NatGeo GTA 3 Sud 1/25k; Fraternali Editore Nos 2, 3 & 4, 1/50k; Blu Edzione Cartoguida 1, 2 & 3
Stages	19

Overview

The southern section of the route covers 19 stages from Castello, south of the Monviso massif to Ventimiglia at the Mediterranean Sea, where you can go no further. South of Castello, the route keeps close to the French border, following the tributaries into the head of Valle Maira, before dropping south and east through the Passo Gardetta to pass by the foot of Rocca la Meja. Moving south through Sambuco, the GTA now visits the highest sanctuary in Europe, that of Sant'Anna, crossing the balcony to Colle della Lombardia. From here the views of the Maritime Alps you are now among are spectacular, but cross the *colle* and you can also look out across the French Mercantour Alps.

Now you head deep into the heart of the Parc Naturale Argentera, to visit the hot springs at Terme di Valdieri before climbing past the base of the Argentera massif itself, a veritable mecca for climbers. Moving east once more, you cross the Colle de Tenda, its pass with 48 hairpin bends a dizzying concept, then through the Parc Valle Tanaro to cross into Liguria, where the trail of the Alta Via Monti Liguri provides a path southward. It is now only a few days easy walking through the Parco delle Alpi Liguri, yet the route keeps to the high ground

until only a cliff descent and 500m of pavement keep
you from the inevitable dip in the ocean.

To Castello

To reach Castello you must take a bus from Saluzzo. Connections to Saluzzo include bus from Turin, taking about 1hr 20min, with Milan a further 50min by train. From Saluzzo the bus runs via Sampeyre to Casteldelfino, Castello and Pontechianle, three times a day (more frequent in school term times), taking about 1hr 15min. From Castello bus stop, it is a short walk back up the road to Rifugio Alevè, although a mention to the driver will likely see you dropped there as the bus passes. Rifugios Grongios Martre and Bagnour are a short walk further on via forest tracks. The next stop further up the road is Pontechinale, another good option for accommodation, especially if you may also need a shop, ATM, pharmacy or other resources. There are campsite options in Pontechianale too, and it is a short walk from here across a footbridge to re-join the route at the west end of Lago di Castello.

From Ventimiglia

Leaving Ventimiglia is straightforward, with a mainline railway station at the foot of the route. The quickest connection to an international airport is by train to Nice, taking about 1hr. A new tramway runs through the town from the port to the airport, taking around 30min and costing just €1.50. A bus from Ventimiglia to Nice is also an option, will be cheaper and is almost as quick. If you need to return via Milan, this is about 3hr 45min by train from Ventimiglia.

STAGE 37

Castello to Rifugio Meleze

Start	Castello (1590m)
Finish	Rifugio Meleze (1812m)
Distance	14.75km
Ascent	1040m
Descent	825m
Time	6hr

A steady climb up through the woods above Lago di Castello affords plenty of views. An old military track makes the descent a gentle one, and the upper Valle Bellino is a wonderful place to take your time exploring the old hamlets of Pleyne and Celle before the final descent to the welcoming Rifugio Meleze.

If you have spent the night at the wonderful Rifugio Alevè, turn right and follow the road uphill into **Castello** itself. Where the road meets the lake (by the bus stop),

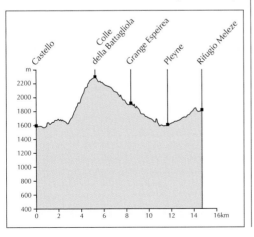

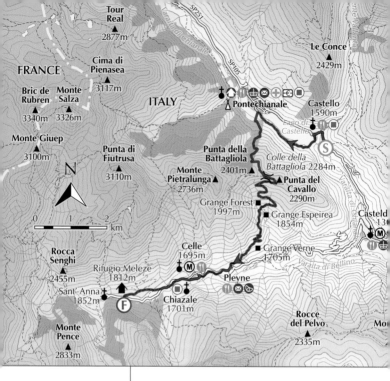

turn left and follow the path across the dam wall above the reservoir. On the far side follow the shoreline trail around to the right, through the trees to the head of the lake. Cross the tributary stream known as Cumbal della Villa, just beyond the head of the lake, where the GTA path turns left alongside an (often dry) stream bed.

> If you need to pick up supplies before you commence the climb, continue up the path a short way and across the bridge into **Frazione Maddalena**, a mostly modern district of Pontechianale. Much of the pretty old district was lost when the valley was dammed and flooded.

Head uphill from the lake, through meadow initially before crossing the stream then climbing more steeply into trees on an obvious trail marked sporadically with red/white blazes on rocks or trees. Continue uphill making use of regular switchbacks as the trees diminish to become alder shrub. As you emerge onto a prominent knoll you can't miss the spectacular view of Monviso if cloud is not down. Continue up the final slope to arrive at **Colle della Battagliola** (2284m).

> A tempting side trail west from the *colle* offers the opportunity to maximise the vantage point from the nearby **Monte Pietralunga** at 2736m. Part-way up a side track to a small top at 2393m is a perfect wild camping spot, flat and sheltered (only a water source is absent) with amazing potential for sunset/sunrise views.

From the *colle*, bear left initially descending on an old military track that contours back and forth in a southerly overall direction.

> A brief excursion from just below the colle to the nearby summit of Punta di Cavallo (2290m) reveals a **monument** to those who perished in the bloody conflict that followed a Franco-Spanish incursion into Piemontese territory in 1744.

At **Grange Espeirea** (1854m) a GTA path forks left past a summer hut, to follow the *torrente* down into Chiesa (1465m). Don't take this route unless you plan to stay in Chiesa. Continue on the main track, crossing the *torrente* and contouring around the hillside, avoiding around 100m of decent and subsequent climb to re-join the GTA at a hairpin on the road just before **Pleyne** (1604m). As you enter Pleyne don't miss the tiny *alimentari* on your left, run from the owner's home. You may need to knock on the door, but the owner is super friendly and it's a great chance to grab some supplies.

Passing through Pleyne you can take the well-marked GTA path which drops off the road between houses and follows a pretty but at times overgrown path to re-join the

Chamois taking flight

road at a bridge below Prafauchier and **Celle** (1695m), or continue up the road through the medieval villages of this quieter fork of the Valle Varaita. Frescoes and sundials feature on many walls amid the ramshackle timber balconies and stone carvings that make excursions into the backstreets here a must. Continuing up the road, the low roof of **Rifugio Meleze** (1812m) soon comes into sight.

FACILITIES INFORMATION FOR STAGE 37

Accommodation

Rifugio Meleze, dormitory, wifi, Pian Melezè, 1, 12020 Bellino, (CN), +39 0175 956410

Casa Alpina Excelsior, mixed rooms, SP256, 12020 Bellino, (CN), +39 0175 956022

Agriturismo Lou Saret, mixed rooms, Borgata Chiazale, 27, 12020 Bellino, (CN), +39 347 975 3899

Trattoria del Pelvo, double and family rooms, wifi, Borgata Chiesa, 40, 12020 Bellino, (CN), +39 0175 956026

Amenities

Meals and limited snacks available at accommodation providers, *alimentari* at Pleyne.

Transport

There is a bus stop at Chiazale and a once a week community bus service runs in the summer into Casteldelfino. In practice a taxi would more than likely be needed to get as far as Casteldelfino, where the bus to Saluzzo runs three times a day taking about 1hr 15min. Connections from Saluzzo include bus to Turin, taking about 1hr 20min, with Milan a further 50min by train.

STAGE 38
Rifugio Meleze to Chiappera

Start	Rifugio Meleze (1812m)
Finish	Chiappera (1622m)
Distance	15.25km
Ascent	1000m
Descent	1160m
Time	6hr 15min

Climb through the valley past the infamous Rocca Senghi to make the ascent to Colle di Bellino, the highest pass on the GTA. This is a fabulous stage, and not too challenging due to the already elevated position of the stage start and end points. The descent into Chiappera is no less dramatic though.

From **Rifugio Meleze**, return to the road and turn right, heading west up the road. Keep left at a fork to the car park at the chapel of **Sant' Anna**. Keep ahead here on a gravel track, crossing the bridge over the stream. Immediately after keep right and cross the second bridge. The obvious track gently climbs amid towering boulders, not least of which the Rocca Senghi on the right cannot be missed. A further bridge crosses the *torrente* at 35min under the shadow of Rocca Senghi as you begin to climb the left side of the valley.

Rocca Senghi, set prominently in the northern slope of the valley head is difficult to miss. The enormous

rock gives the impression of a full sail in the wind and is the source of much local legend.

Follow the trail markings and clear path alongside the steep banks of the *torrente* and continue to reach the flat pasture basin of **Grange dell'Autaret** (2547m). Turn left here at a signpost marked for Colle di Bellino. Ascend the grass slope initially then onto bare scree, where you can encounter snow patches well into summer. Climb the final incline to reach **Colle di Bellino** (2804m).

A 30min excursion up **Monte Bellino** (2937m) is well worth the small amount of extra effort on a clear day for an outstanding viewpoint of the surrounding mountains. The view north is dominated by the southern end of the Monviso ridge, a dark pyramid which stands clear above all else. North-west is Monte Maniglia (3177m) a prominent marker on the French border. East-north-east is the razor-sharp ridge of Pelvo d'Elva (3064m), while south-west the ridge that marks the French border is dominated by Brec de Chambeyorn (3388m).

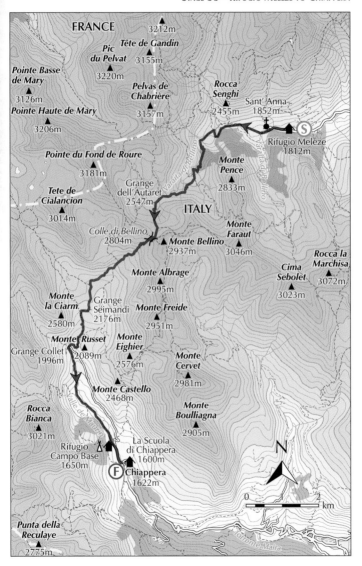

215

Monviso from the summit of Monte Bellino

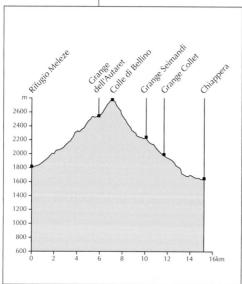

From the *colle* descend broadly ahead south-west by way of switchbacks and a dusty track among eroded ridges. Descend the grassy slope down the middle of the valley initially, with imposing crags on either side and the vast green basin ahead enclosed by an amphitheatre of impressive spires. Gradually crossing to the right side of the valley, the path becomes somewhat indistinct amid a mass of cattle tracks and there is a dearth of markings, however a general bearing south sees a couple of small ponds come into view and beyond you soon reach the military road that now serves the farm at **Grange Seimandi** (2176m). Follow this down as it switches back and forth amid rocks. Note that the National Geographic mapping now shows a slightly different route into Chiappera than earlier maps, staying high from Grange Semandi, to cross the Colle Greguri. This guide has retained the original route as it directly passes Campo Base where many choose to stay. If staying at La Scuola in the heart of Chiappera then the National Geographic marked route offers a high-level alternate.

Ignore several side tracks and keep left past the summer farm at **Grange Collet** (1996m) and around the back of the grassy knoll with the *torrente* gushing clear and inviting on your left. Descend around the contour and ahead crossing the bigger vehicle track. Continue now with the *torrente* in a deeper gorge on your left. Keeping on the main track continue past the impressive Stroppia waterfall on your right and on past a campsite on your left. It is now just a short stroll ahead to **Rifugio Campo Base** (1650m) up the ramp on the right, and a little further down the track to reach **Chiappera** (1622m).

FACILITIES INFORMATION FOR STAGE 38

Accommodation

Rifugio Campo Base, mixed rooms, wifi, Frazione Chiappera, 12021 Chiappera, (CN), +39 334 841 6041

Ospitalità Montana La Scuola di Chiappera, double and family rooms, wifi, Borgata Chiappera, 78, 12021 Acceglio, (CN), +39 334 767 0616

Amenities

Meals and limited snacks available at accommodation providers.

Transport

A community shuttle bus (Sherpa Bus – ask at accommodation providers) can be booked as far as Acceglio to connect with a regular bus to Dronero and if desired an onward bus to Cuneo to meet rail connections.

STAGE 39
Chiappera to Rifugio della Gardetta

Start	Chiappera (1622m)
Finish	Rifugio della Gardetta (2335m)
Distance	17km
Ascent	1245m
Descent	555m
Time	7hr

A lovely stage climbing through open woodland with sporadic views of surrounding mountains. The gradient is often gentle to begin, with short steeper sections before the climb to the first *colle* begins in earnest, still in the shade of the trees. Old military roads ensure an easy descent and way marking is clear. World War 2 bunkers add interest to the second climb before a short descent in the shadow of Rocca la Meja.

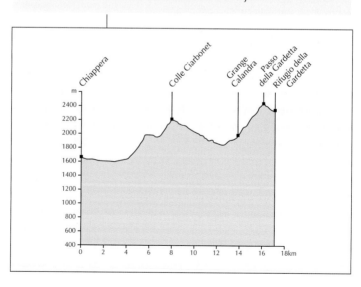

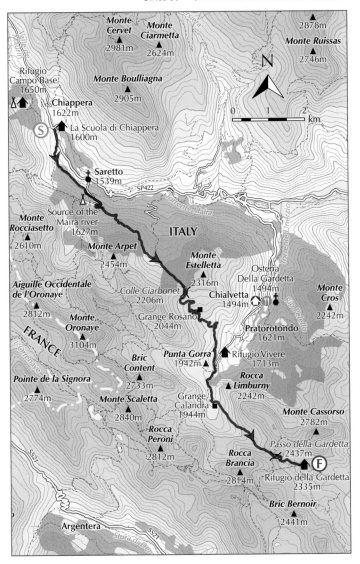

Whether from **Rifugio Campo Base** or already in the heart of **Chiappera**, take the road south initially, continuing to a hairpin bend where the trail leaves the road on the right. At a fork in the path keep left and continue through pleasant woodland. Keep ahead, ignoring a couple of further side paths as you walk on, or to the side of, a concrete-covered aquifer with occasional refreshing sounds of water gushing beneath your feet. Keep left at a signposted fork then, as you emerge onto the small road keep ahead uphill, around the corner and through the main entrance to the campsite at the **source of the Maira river** (Sorgenti del Maira, 1627m). Bear immediately left uphill into more woodland to take the first track junction on your left on a smaller path. A long but pleasant, undulating climb ensues through open woodland and successive clearings to a track junction, the trail has recently been rerouted here to minimise erosion, and the change is not yet reflected on some maps but is clearly marked on the ground. Bear left across a small log bridge over a swampy section and continue uphill largely parallel to the original path. Red/white blazes sporadically on trees or rocks continue to mark the way. In the upper reaches of the trees more clearings open up, abundant with wildflowers, after which you emerge quite suddenly from the trees, on the **Colle Ciarbonet** (2206m).

Turn right for the descent from the *colle* which takes advantage of an old military track, that you will follow for around the next hour. Descending in a broadly southeast direction, the multiple switchbacks keep the gradient gentle.

Eventually you reach a road end at a switchback, below the conical peak of Punta Gorra (1942). Keep right here at a signpost for Passo della Gardetta. The left here would take you past the delightful Rifugio Vivere, out to Chialvetta where alternative accommodation can be found. The track climbs gently alongside the upper reaches of the Torrente Unerzio crossing over to the left bank before reaching **Grange Calandra** (1944m) where the GTA leaves the track. Turn left here and follow the smaller path uphill, passing fascinating old military

bunkers, until you reach **Passo della Gardetta** (2437m) from where Rifugio della Gardetta comes into view, stood alone in the vast plain at the foot of the impressive Rocca la Meja. Cross over the pass and take the left onto a further military track that descends to reach **Rifugio della Gardetta** (2335m).

Military bunker below Passo della Gardetta

> **Rocca la Meja** is an impressive pyramidal peak of 2840m, sat in the Meja-Gardetta plateau, in the Cottian Alps. Unsurprisingly popular due to its height and relative isolation on the surrounding plain, many people visit to walk the Rocca la Meja loop. A circuit of 13.4km, the route typically takes about 6hr with an ascent and descent of around 700m.

FACILITIES INFORMATION FOR STAGE 39

Accommodation

Osteria della Gardetta, mixed rooms, wifi, Borgo Chialvetta, 12, 12021 Acceglio (CN), +39 0171 99017

Rifugio Vivere, mixed rooms, wifi, Borgata Viviere, 12021 Acceglio, (CN), +39 0171 164 5470

Rifugio della Gardetta, dormitory, Pianoro di Pianezzo, 12020 Canosio, (CN), +39 348 238 0158

Note: Rifugio della Gardetta is popular especially at weekends and during the August holidays. Booking in advance is always required.

Amenities
Meals and limited snacks available at accommodation providers.

Transport
None on route.

STAGE 40
Rifugio della Gardetta to Sambuco

Start	Rifugio della Gardetta (2335m)
Finish	Sambuco (1280m)
Distance	19.5km
Ascent	480m
Descent	1645m
Time	7hr

Dominated by the Rocca la Meja, the early part of this stage allows a close-up view of this peak, taking in part of the popular circuit trek. Beyond, the military tracks facilitate easy walking across this high-level plateau amid gorgeous mountain tops. The descent is no less enjoyable, following a tree-lined gorge to the beautiful and historic hamlet of Sambuco.

Leaving **Rifugio della Gardetta**, turn right, following the track south-east. The track loops to a junction where you turn left to continue in a south-easterly direction, however, most will cut the corner on the smaller path. A short way beyond, leave the track at a high point below crags and keep ahead on a smaller path. Keep left of a grassy knoll to shortcut the track and re-join it further on, rising

now to the **Col del Preit** (2076m) where the **Agriturismo La Meja** provides basic accommodation. Turn right here and follow the track, across the *torrente* and around the hill, cross a second *torrente* and reach Gias della Margherina (2169m).

Rocca la Meja under a stormy sky

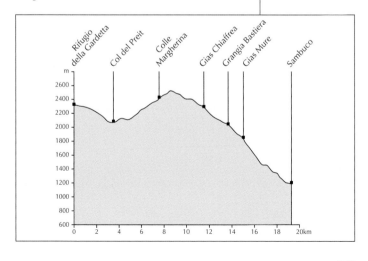

223

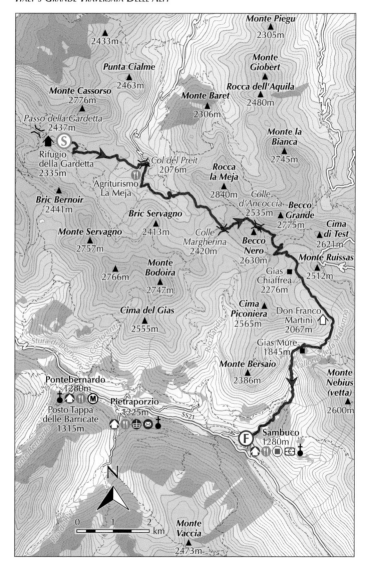

Continue on a smaller path, keeping left of the farm buildings to climb to a track junction then bear right climbing and traversing below the lower scree slopes of Rocca la Meja. After bearing left and climbing more steeply, the path forks. Keep right to reach **Colle Margherina** (2420m). Don't cross but turn left here and ascend the gentle slope to pass Lago della Meja, then at a track junction follow the main track round to the right to cross **Colle d'Ancoccia** (2535m) between Becco Grande and Becco Nero. Descend ahead through a switchback to a fork. Keep left here and proceed to a crossroads in the track. Turn right here and descend to Vallo Alpino (2418m). Keep round to the right now and then sharply left at the next turn just before the military ruins of Caserme Della Bandia (2403m). Follow the track as it bears right, around a rocky promontory, then keep right at the junction, where an alternate GTA path joins the track. At a corner drop down the bank to shortcut the track as it loops out to huts at **Gias Chiaffrea**, then re-join it for a long gradual descent parallel to the *torrente* to reach **Rifugio Don Franco Martini** (2067m).

> **Rifugio Don Franco Martini** is a self-catering hut with a communal room, small kitchen, bathroom and sleeping loft. It is kept locked, but keys can be obtained from the *trattoria* La Meridiana in Sambuco (+39 0171 96650)

Continue downhill bearing right to follow the *torrente*, past the huts at Gias Sale and **Gias Mure** (1845m) where a prominent shrine sits alongside the track on a grassy knoll that marks the beginning of the steeper descent. Continue down the narrowing tree-lined gorge on an easily followed track, keeping the *torrente* on your right all the way down. Ignore a couple of side tracks and emerge from the trees to cross a wooden bridge onto a vehicle track. Turn left here and follow the track down into **Sambuco**. Keep right at the junction by a water fountain in Sambuco to reach the main square and *albergo*.

FACILITIES INFORMATION FOR STAGE 40

Accommodation

Agriturismo La Meja, simple rooms, Colle del Preit, 12020 Canosio, (CN), +39 0171 998116

Albergo Ristorante della Pace, double and twin rooms, wifi, Via Umberto I, 32/34, 12010 Sambuco, (CN), +39 0171 96550

B&B Radici Sambuco, double rooms, wifi, via campanile, 6, 12010 Sambuco, (CN), +39 328 809 1436

Amenities

Meals and limited snacks available at accommodation providers.

Transport

A bus operates five times a day from Sambuco to Vinadio (20min), where a change enables a bus to Cuneo (1hr 5min) to connect with train services.

STAGE 41
Sambuco to Strepeis

Start	Sambuco (1280m)
Finish	Strepeis (1275m)
Distance	11km
Ascent	1140m
Descent	1035m
Time	5hr 30min

The climb from Sambuco is through the shade of trees until the higher slopes where grass begins to dominate. After the steeper final stretch, the brow of the hill comes suddenly, and the open, airy plateau atop the *colle* is a pleasure to linger on, exploring the remains of the fort here. The descent is full of interest too, not least the lovely little hamlet of Bagni di Vinadio.

Leave the square in **Sambuco** heading west, along the small lane between buildings, past the ATM and downhill to the main road. Cross the main road and continue down the small road opposite to cross the *torrente*. On the far side of the bridge a sign on the wall guides you right for a short distance where a footpath leaves the road left, steeply up into the woods. Take this and climb through switchbacks to a second small road where a convenient picnic bench enables a rest alongside the path. The climb is not as steep as

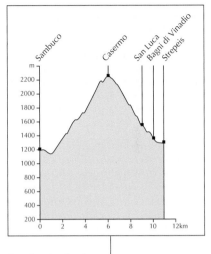

it initially appears. Passing a hut housing the Sambuco community aqueduct keep left ignoring the side trail. The long climb is in and out of the trees with a couple of false summits before emerging onto the open shoulder of Monte Vaccia and past the remains of military barracks (**Casermo** 2243m).

Casermo di Monte Vaccia

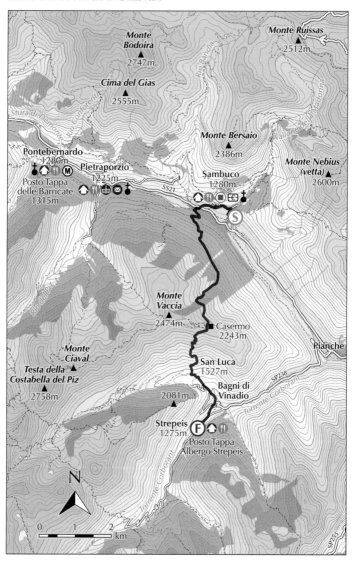

Monte Ruissas
2512m.

Monte
Bodoira
2747m.

Cima del Gias
2555m

Monte Bersaio
2386m.

Pontebernardo
1280m
Pietraporzio
1225m

Monte Nebius
(vetta)
2600m.

Sambuco
1280m.

Posto Tappa
delle Barricate
1315m

Monte
Vaccia
2474m.

Casermo
2243m

Pianche

Monte
Ciaval

Testa della
Costabella del Piz
2758m.

San Luca
1527m

Bagni di
Vinadio

2081m.

Strepeis
1275m
Posto Tappa
Albergo Strepeis

N

0   1   2
km

Continue ahead past the old barracks to a track junction marked with a signpost. Continue beyond this then follow the contour to the right to begin the steep descent. The path is largely under trees now, on a carpet of pine cones and needles for much of the way, on short, steep switchbacks. As the trees thin significantly, you will reach a track by a clearing. Turn left here and descend to houses at **San Luca** (1527m), passing through a narrow passageway onto the grass beyond where you will find a giant ant sculpture called Leone, playing a violin!

Just beyond this follow the marked route right and downhill somewhat back on yourself. The path beyond descends through haymeadow and wildflowers before dropping once again into the shade of the trees.

Ignoring side turnings, cross the *torrente* and continue on the track with the *torrente* on your left. Reaching a road hairpin, keep left, for around 100m where just beyond a sharp right bend, take the small signed track off to the left steeply down through trees with a drop to the *torrente* gully on your left. Ignore the fork that switches back to your left and continue between houses and descend the cobbled path through upper **Bagni di Vinadio**. Where the steps begin keep right then turn ninety degrees right around the corner of a house to emerge into the square by the church and water fountain. Across the square pick up the gravel track south-west signed for Strepeis. At the main road turn right and walk ahead into **Strepeis** (1275m). The *posto tappa* is on your left, keys from the *albergo* a little further on, on the right.

FACILITIES INFORMATION FOR STAGE 41

Accommodation

Lou Loop B&B, double rooms, wifi, Frazione Bagni, 59, 12010 Vinadio, (CN), +39 347 145 2505

Albergo Nasi, double and twin rooms, wifi, Via Maestra, 35, 12010 Vinadio, (CN), +39 0171 95834

Posto Tappa Albergo Strepeis, dormitory and rooms, wifi, Frazione Strepeis, 16, 12010 Vinadio, (CN), +39 0171 95831

Amenities
Meals and limited snacks available at accommodation providers.

Transport
None on route.

STAGE 42
Strepeis to Rifugio Malinvern

Start	Strepeis (1275m)
Finish	Rifugio Malinvern (1836m)
Distance	21.25km
Ascent	1830m
Descent	1300m
Time	9hr

This long stage can be broken down with a stay at the fascinating Santuario di Sant' Anna di Vinadio for those who prefer a shorter day. However, long stretches of easier walking enable plenty of ground to be covered and Rifugio Malinvern is within reach for the energetic. A pleasant climb is followed by open and undulating ground to the *santuario*, then a brief climb to a long ridge which leads to the Colle della Lombarda. Finally, there is a short, if rocky, climb before a gentler forest descent ends the stage.

From **Strepeis**, head south across the gravel parking area to cross the old wooden bridge over the river and turn left to follow the track downstream. Keep left at the first fork, then bear right at the next, signposted GTA, turning sharply right at a corner to climb alongside the tributary *torrente* under pleasant deciduous tree cover. After

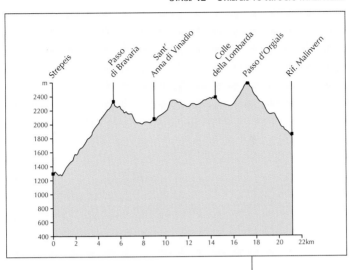

around an hour cross the *torrente* to the left bank, leaving the trees now, and continue towards the head of the valley. At a small fork keep left, to climb away from the now diminishing *torrente*. Cross the high pasture basin, dotted with Arolla pines, to reach the **Passo di Bravaria** (2311m).

Passing from the lush greens of the northern slopes of Rocca Bravaria to those south facing, the contrast is stark. The steeper south side is bare and scree-strewn, so care must be taken initially. Descend south, steeply down at first, then undulating as you traverse the slope among shrubs and the hardier trees that cling on here. Continue across the slope for some way to reach the **Santuario di Sant'Anna di Vinadio** (2035m), and **Rifugio San Gioachino**.

Leave the *santuario*, crossing in front of the restaurant, and keep right at the fork following the road uphill. Continue ahead between the upper gravel car park and the statue of the Madonna on a rock, the now obvious path continues up the hillside. Ignore two possible side turnings and stay on the main track as you climb. Only once you reach the Lago del Colle di Sant'Anna do you

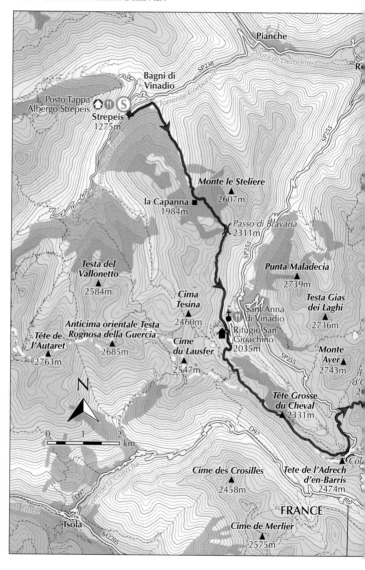

fork left on a smaller track now signed GTA, Rifugio Malinvern and Colle della Lombarda. The climb steepens towards the ridge and after a final push you arrive on a grassy knoll with views across the French–Italian border that you now follow to the **Colle della Lombarda** (2351m) where motorcycles gather and riders pose for photos alongside the road sign, covered in the club stickers of thousands of bike clubs from around the world.

A faint path can be followed here to avoid the first section of road walking from the *colle*. Stepping down from the road to the second switchback on the gravel track below, the path can be found heading north across grassy terrain. If this cannot be

Passo d'Orgials
2600m

233

found, simply continue around the road to find the sign-post marked GTA on the right, on a left-bearing bend in the road. Turn right here and climb the rocky but clear path, keeping right at a fork part-way to reach the **Passo d'Orgials** (2600m).

The descent is as rocky as the climb. Watch out for the chamois that frequent the craggy slopes either side as you descend from the *colle*. Switchbacks lessen the gradient, but care is still required. Pass the plateau of the Laghi d'Orgials then descend again to a further, smaller plateau and lake. After a short climb over the left ridge, begin the final descent through lush shrub, damp underfoot at times as the stream and path intertwine. In the final 100m ignore a tempting left and stay ahead across rocky boulders to emerge by **Rifugio Malinvern** (1836m).

FACILITIES INFORMATION FOR STAGE 42

Accommodation

Rifugio San Gioachino, double and family rooms, 12010 Vinadio, Province of Cuneo, +39 0171 959125

Rifugio Malinvern, mixed rooms, wifi, Vallone Di Rio Freddo Snc, 12010 Vinadio, (CN), +39 0171 193 6018

Amenities

Meals and limited snacks available at accommodation providers and simple lunches available in a café/bar at the santuario.

Transport

None on route.

STAGE 43

Rifugio Malinvern to Terme di Valdieri

Start	Rifugio Malinvern (1836m)
Finish	Terme de Valdieri (1368m)
Distance	13.5km
Ascent	745m
Descent	1180m
Time	5hr 30min

A beautiful and shorter stage that takes you from the far-reaching views of the Colletto di Valscura, down past sparkling lakes and historic military remains for the opportunity to relax in the thermal pools for which the valley is famed.

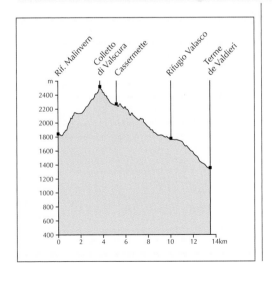

Head across the yard in front of **Rifugio Malinvern** to pick up the small, signed track ahead marked 'GTA, Terme de Valdieri'. Follow this to the *torrente* and across a log bridge to begin the climb back and forth up the steep-sided valley. After around 1hr, skirt around to the right side of the **Lago Malinvern**, amid gorgeous views of surrounding peaks. The path ahead is visible climbing up scree on the far side. Follow the path up through short switchbacks becoming steeper towards the *colle*. Late-lying snow is common on this north-facing side. The **Colletto di Valscura** (2520m) rewards with stunning views across glistening lakes to the Argentera massif.

The descent into the Valle di Valasco is a series of steps through lake-filled upper valleys, scattered with old military fortifications. Cross the *colle* and descend the narrow path that switches back and forth across the scree slope to reach the Lago inferiore di Valscura. Ignore the

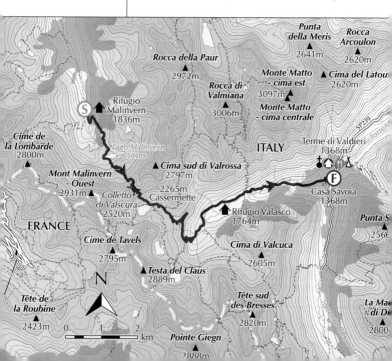

Trail through the military tunnel

path right and keep left past a series of ruined fortifications, barracks (**Cassermette**, 2265m) and outbuildings, then pick your way across the lake outflow. Continue ahead now down the old military road. A series of solidly built stone supporting walls guide the road around successive tight bends. On your left as the view opens up you can also see the dark opening of the tunnel through which the old military road passes. You have the choice to take this gentle incline, tunnel and switchback (recommended) or to use the steeper path to the right to drop onto the lower road.

A little way beyond the tunnel, pass the side track on the right marked for 'Rifugio E. Questa (2388m)', followed by a series of tight switchbacks that drop you down to the beautiful hanging valley and pasture basin below, in the centre of which sits the intriguing **Rifugio Valasco** (1764m), passing several beautiful waterfalls on the way. Beyond Valasco, follow the wide stony track alongside the river for around 15min, staying on the main track. Ignore the solidly built wooden steps that appear on the right, but go a little further and look out for and take the footpath that slopes away to the right to travel alongside the *torrente* avoiding multiple road hairpins. This path is not marked GTA, but is the most direct and more pleasant route into Terme di Valdieri. Emerge alongside the camping site and take either a small path to the right or follow the road to your left into the centre. Albergo Turismo is on your left and the posto tappa at **Casa Savoia** a little further on.

> The sulphurous thermal springs at **Terme di Valdieri** date back to at least the mid-16th century when the first Spa complex was built by the municipality. In 1755 King Carlo Emanuele III visited and the grand building that is now the hotel was built for the occasion. Despite a devastating fire and subsequent reconstruction, the place thrived and when in 1855 King Vittorio Emanuele visited, the Royal Hunting Reserve was born.

FACILITIES INFORMATION FOR STAGE 43

Accommodation

Rifugio Valasco, mixed rooms, wifi, Loc. Piano del Valasco, 12010 Valdieri, (CN), +39 0171 183 6267

Albergo Turismo, double and twin rooms, wifi, Regione Terme, 3, 12010 Terme di Valdieri, (CN), +39 340 142 3408

Casa Savoia, mixed rooms, Regione Terme, 1, 12010 Valdieri, (CN), +39 327 011 6545

Amenities

Meals and limited snacks available at accommodation providers.

Transport

None on route.

STAGE 44

Terme di Valdieri to Rifugio Genova-Figari

Start	Terme de Valdieri (1368m)
Finish	Rifugio Genova-Figari (2010m)
Distance	14km
Ascent	1255m
Descent	635m
Time	6hr 15min

An exciting stage dominated by close views of the Argentera, a magnet for local climbers. The crags of this valley are home to the fascinating ibex, too. Despite the wild and remote feel to the stage, the climb and descent are eased by well-maintained tracks and switchbacks, and the wonderful Rifugio Morrelli Buzzi makes for an excellent lunch break.

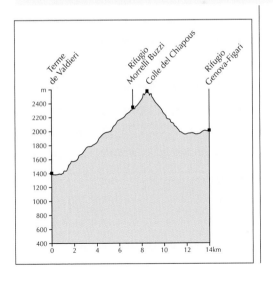

Lago del Chiotas

With the Hotel Royal on your right and the thermal pools on your left, head downhill and out through the iron gates. Continue across the junction to a gravel car park where the old *mulattiera* can be found on the right, climbing south-east up the Vallone di Lourousa. Turn right onto the GTA path (signposted) here and commence the ascent sheltered by mixed woodland on a gradient aided by multiple switchbacks. Emerging from the trees, the route becomes rockier, the scree and boulders seeming to have fallen from the Argentera itself, the imposing rock massif that dominates the views on your right all the way to the *colle*.

As you climb you can scarcely ignore the glistening white streak of the infamous ice gully of **Canalone Lourousa**, popular among climbers and route of the first ever ascent. The prominent top to the right of the cluser is Corno Stella (3050m), beyond and to the left of the ice gully is Monte Stella at 3282m.

Pass Lagarot di Lourousa just off the path down the slope to the right. More of a wide, slow section of the stream than a lake, it is nonetheless a fabulous place to dangle hot feet in the water while enjoying the views. Forty minutes or so further on the small side excursion to **Rifugio Morrelli Buzzi** (2351m) is reached. This tiny Rifugio is as intriguing as the food is good. You may spot the beautiful hand-made accordions, these are the work of the proprietor. Evenings can become quite musical. Certainly worth a lunch stop even if you don't plan to stay the night. The climb from the *rifugio* winds its way upward through a boulder field. Then continue to follow

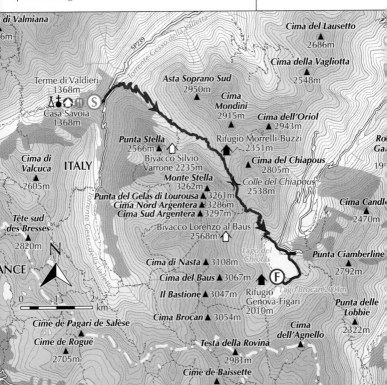

the painted blazes back and forth to reach the **Colle del
Chiapous** (2538m).

The descent begins gradually as the path picks its way
through scree and rock, across to the right initially passing the rock-strewn basin just beyond the *colle*. Ignoring
the small side track here (to the Bivacco Lorenzo al Baus,
2568m), the descent proper commences just below the
intriguingly named Passo del Porco (2580m), literally
the 'step of the pig'. A well-maintained path makes light
work of the otherwise steep slope angle and the going is
never difficult, while views of the surrounding mountains
and reservoir (in Italian a *bacino artificiale*) below distract
from an otherwise uneventful descent.

As you reach the reservoir (usually referred to locally
as lake or 'Lago' del Chiotas), cross the first dam wall
and then keep left, passing to the rear of the massive rock
on which sits a control building. The service road will
take you down below the second dam wall and through
a small tunnel to emerge on the far side. A signed gravel
ramp immediately on the right takes you back up to
above the reservoir water level. Now follow the service
road around the reservoir. Note the signed side-trail for

Colle di Fenestrelle on your left, this will be your route as you commence the next stage in the morning. Ten minutes further round the reservoir and you reach the **Rifugio Genova-Figari** (2010m).

THE LARGEST PUMPED-STORAGE HYDRO-ELECTRIC PLANT IN EUROPE

The former Rifugio Genova (1914m) was once the oldest alpine club hut in the Maritime Alps, dating from 1898. That ended in the 1970s when the electricity company Enel flooded the upper valley, in which the famous *rifugio* sat, as part of an ambitious hydro-electric project. The scheme commenced in 1969 with the creation of Lago del Rovina in the lower valley and came to fruition in 1982, when the new plant began production. The pumping station on the central rock looks over the 130m high dam wall which retains over 27 million m³ of water at its peak water level of 1978m.

Part of the deal with Enel was the construction of a new purpose-built mountain hut to replace the historic structure submerged below the dark waters of the reservoir. Construction began in 1979, and in 1981 the new Rifugio Genova-Figari opened at 2010m situated atop a prominent crag overlooking the reservoir at the foot of the Argentera. Surrounded by impressive peaks, the location is as much a mecca for climbers as it is a haven for wildlife. A glance outside at dusk can see ibex rutting on the boulders above the lake, chamois grazing behind the *rifugio* and marmots scurrying amongst the rocks.

FACILITIES INFORMATION FOR STAGE 44

Accommodation

Rifugio Morelli-Buzzi, mixed rooms, Vallone di Lourousa, 12010 Valdieri, (CN), +39 0171 97394

Rifugio Genova-Figari, mixed rooms, Strada Comunale Rovine, 12010 Entracque, (CN), +39 340 461 4189

Amenities

Meals and limited snacks available at accommodation providers.

Transport

None on route.

STAGE 45
Rifugio Genova-Figari to San Giacomo

Start	Rifugio Genova-Figari (2010m)
Finish	San Giacomo (1225m)
Distance	11.25km
Ascent	465m
Descent	1240m
Time	4hr 30min

In many ways this is a simple stage of up, down and along, but that would suggest it didn't have great interest and it certainly does. The viewpoint on the Argentera from the *colle* is superb, and in descent the peaks on your right are the boundary with France hinting at the Mercantour Alps beyond. The area around the *colle* is also a fantastic spot to see the ancient-looking ibex, their long horns often visible on the skyline.

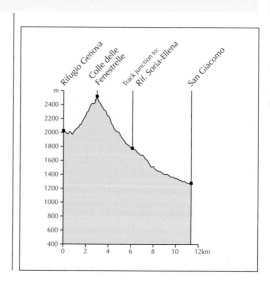

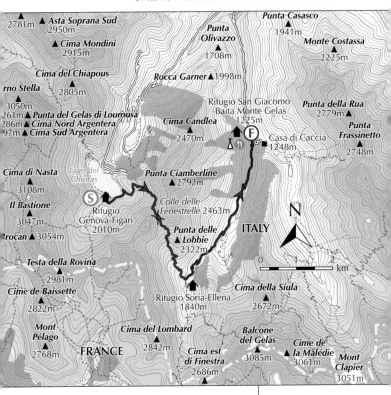

Follow the track back around the lake, to the signposted side track heading south-east uphill to the *colle*. It is a straightforward climb first under the crags of Rocce di Laura, then climbing around the hill to reach the **Colle delle Fenestrelle** (2463m), nestled under the conical Punta Fenestrelle (2701m). The broad *colle* retains late-lying snow for a considerable time, but being relatively level, it's not difficult to cross. The descent begins gradually then steepens, making extensive use of switchbacks to ease the gradient. A little way beyond the *colle*, pass the remains of a military outpost. Now ibex and chamois are the most frequent visitors here.

Bee hives are a common sight outside mountain villages

Rock and scree continue most of the way down the slope, although the grassy knoll of Punta Delle Lobbie (2322m) provides the opportunity to rest the knees. Further down, the slope lessens and shortly after, a track junction (1790m) is reached. Here, across and right you can see the Rifugio Soria-Ellena (1840m), but our route turns left to take the broad gravel track that follows the Torrente Gesso della Barra down the long valley to **San Giacomo** and the **Rifugio San Giacomo-Baita Monte Gelas** (1225m).

San Giacomo is an Italian translation of St James, and the *foresteria* a former lodging on the important pilgrimage route leading over the Colle di Finestra, to the Madone de Fenestre an important pilgrimage sanctuary at an altitude of 1903m in the Mercantour Alps. The route continues as the Way of St James that terminates at Santiago de Compostela.

FACILITIES INFORMATION FOR STAGE 45

Accommodation

Rifugio Soria-Ellena, mixed rooms, Pian del Praiet, 12010 San Giacomo di Entracque, Valle Gesso, (CN), +39 0171 978382

Rifugio San Giacomo-Baita Monte Gelas, dormitory, wifi (at the restaurant opposite), Frazione San Giacomo, 12010 Entracque, (CN), +39 0171 978704

Seasonal campsite at San Giacomo.

Amenities

Meals and limited snacks available at accommodation providers. Food and drinks at Baita Monte Gelas in San Giacomo, and the seasonal campsite also operates a take-away food bar.

Transport

None on route.

STAGE 46
San Giacomo to Trinita

Start	San Giacomo (1225m)
Finish	Trinita (1091m)
Distance	11km
Ascent	730m
Descent	865m
Time	4hr 45min

An option presents itself on this stage, to travel directly to Trinita, or with a little extra road walking, travel slightly further to visit Entracque. If supplies are needed, this is certainly a straightforward extension and there is a good *alimentari* in the town. It extends the walk to around 14km, but reduces the climb to about 550m. Also worth a visit is the wolf and man visitor centre in Entracque, where the challenges and opportunities of wolf reintroduction into the mountains are presented and explored. At the end of the route Locanda del Sorisso is a comfortable stay with excellent local food.

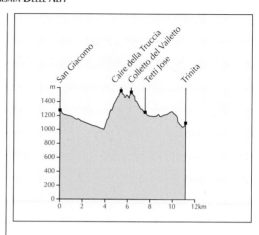

Leaving **San Giacomo**, head down the road for a short distance and turn right across the bridge, then take the track left alongside the extensive camping area. Continue beyond the campsite to the *torrente*, keeping this on your left and the woods on your right. Continue past a hut at **Tetto Terapin** (1135m), over a tributary and further on the far bank, Tetto Tanasso, the stream now becoming a gorge. As the gorge broadens, opposite a footbridge, ◀ take a right turn onto a small signposted path that follows a tributary stream uphill into the woods. After around 400m of climb bear left as the path climbs past a viewpoint at **Caire della Truccia** (1572m). The path continues north-east crossing over the **Colletto del Vailetto** (1500m) below the north ridge of Punta Casasco (1941m), then descending to become a broader track.

The alternate via Entracque crosses the brdge here.

Continue a short way now to huts at **Tetti Jose** (1241m) on the left. Just beyond a turning on the right is signposted 'Tetti d'Ambrin'. Turn right here for the shortest route around the slope to re-join the marked GTA track and turn right. (Rifugio Esterate is a short way down the track to the left).

Note that some maps show the GTA continuing beyond **Tetti Jose**, all the way to the church at Tetto

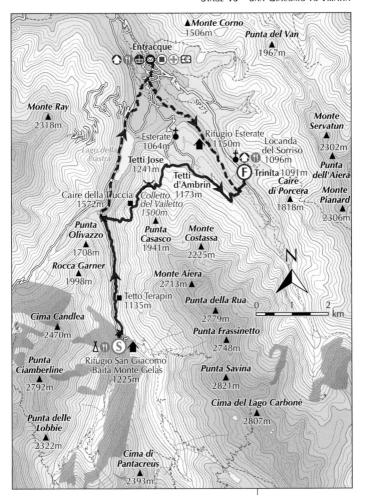

Airetta, then turning sharply right to head up the valley on a broad track. The route across proposed here merely shortcuts that longer way to re-join the same track.

Lizards basking on a rock

Continue south-east to the end of the broad track and turn left following a smaller path down the short slope, across a further track and over a wooden bridge across the *torrente*. Climb the slope on the far side then bear left around and then alongside a garden to pass under an arch between houses onto the road. Turn left here and find the cosy **Locanda del Sorriso** (1096m) on your right.

Alternate route

To go into Entracque, take the footpath as far as the footbridge then cross to the west bank of the torrente, and take the road north alongside the reservoir. Turn off the road into the Enel Hydroelectric visitor centre and cross the grass verge to the lower road that runs under the dam wall. This can be followed into Entracque, however a shorter route is possible by taking the track north from this road across scrub and pasture, eventually over a *torrente* on a footbridge, left and then a lane behind buildings to join the end of the road 'Vicolo Caire'. On the way out, take Strada Via Sartaria from Entracque signed Trinita 1hr 45min. This becomes a gravel track, and travels all the way to the footbridge below Locanda del Sorriso.

STAGE 47 – TRINITA TO PALANFRÈ

FACILITIES INFORMATION FOR STAGE 46

Accommodation

Rifugio Esterate, double and twin rooms, wifi, Strada Comunale Esterate, 12010 tetti Cilia, località Esterate, (CN), +39 347 881 7137

Locanda del Sorriso, mixed rooms, wifi, Strada Provinciale per Trinità, 12010 Trinità, (CN), +39 0171 978388

Amenities

Meals and limited snacks available at accommodation providers.

Extension to Entracque offers access to groceries, pharmacy, an ATM and sports shop.

Transport

None on main route.

From Entracque a direct bus to Cuneo (35min) runs four times a day.

STAGE 47
Trinita to Palanfrè

Start	Trinita (1091m)
Finish	Palanfrè (1379m)
Distance	10.5km
Ascent	1105m
Descent	810m
Time	5hr

Commencing among trees, and climbing initially alongside a *torrente*, this route quickly gains height and with it, views. A fabulous, lofty ridge walk precedes a descent through dense wildflower meadows ending at a wonderful family run trattoria and Rifugio.

Leaving **Trinita**, walk ahead down the street a short way then turn right. Head up the street, towards **Tetti Prer**, then keep right at the fork onto a track. Around 20min up the track the path forks again (signposted), keep left here, on the smaller track for a short distance before reaching a *torrente*. The path ascends alongside with cables providing security on rock and shale that can become slippery when wet. Shady hazel woodland follows, then another rocky patch. The trees are left behind shortly before you reach the broad grassy shoulder of the Caire di Porcera (1818m). Here turn left and follow the path continuing up to the left of the grassy knoll, then right to traverse the slope.

As you reach the next shoulder ridge, turn left again for a steeper section then follow the track to the right and up to reach **Colle della Garbella** (2170m). Bear right and commence a glorious ridge walk for around 1km. As you begin to descend from the ridge on the left side, a

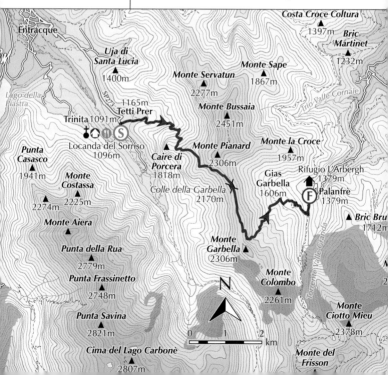

couple of large switchbacks bring you gradually around to a north-east direction. The descent through wildflower pasture is pleasant but can become overgrown in early season.

Entracque from the colle

The trail moves to the right of the valley and finds its way onto a small ridge then down a ramp onto the vehicle track below. Turn right here, downhill, then keep left at the fork.

From here continue to follow the track downhill, ignoring side paths. As you near Palanfrè a signpost marks the track right to Limonetto and Passo di Ciotto Mien, note this in preparation for commencing the next stage, but for now continue left down the track to **Palanfrè** (1379m). The **Rifugio l'Arbergh** is up some stone steps on the left.

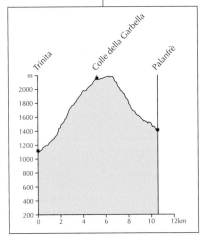

FACILITIES INFORMATION FOR STAGE 47

Accommodation
Rifugio l'Arbergh, double and twin rooms, wifi, Strada Palanfrè, 19, 12019 Vernante, (CN), +39 349 327 0733

Amenities
Meals and limited snacks available at accommodation provider.

Transport
None on route.

STAGE 48
Palanfrè to Limonetto

Start	Palanfrè (1379m)
Finish	Limonetto (1294m)
Distance	10.5km
Ascent	865m
Descent	970m
Time	4hr 45min

A shorter stage that enables a gentle start through lush woodland, giving way to shrub and wildflowers as height is gained. The *colle* feels dramatic and rewarding, steep and rocky on one side, then quickly onto comfortable ground again in descent. A good gradient allows the ground to be covered quickly and an early finish enables time for exploring. Limonetto itself is mostly a small and fairly dull ski resort, but a short bus ride into Limone Piemonte gives access to a better range of stores and facilities.

Leaving the wonderful *rifugio* at **Palanfrè**, proceed back up the hill for a couple of minutes to the track junction signposted for Passo di Ciotto Mien and take the left here on a pleasant woodland path. After around 20min keep right at the fork. Some way beyond at a signed track junction keep right (although either option is a loop returning to the main track). Just a little further on you will find a wonderfully placed piped spring that emerges from a rock on the right of the path, followed by huts at **Gias Piamian** (1635m). Bearing left at the next junction, and climbing more steeply now, reach a clear but sporadically marked path to **Lago degli Alberghi** (2032m). A small path cuts the corner to continue, but it is worth climbing right up to the lake outflow where a level spot among boulders invites rest and contemplation.

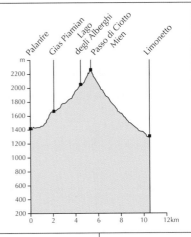

From the lake follow the track, bearing left directly up the slope then traversing across to the right for the climb to the *colle*, becoming steeper in the final stretch where a

Lago degli Alberghi

Chain handrail on Passo di Ciotto Mien

Monte Bussaia
2451m

Monte Malaterra
1426m

Monte
la Croce
1957m

onte Pianard
2306m

Mo
Mt
154

Monte Vecchio
1919m

Rifugio
L'Arbergh
1379m

Palanfrè
1379m

Bric Castea
1800m

Limone
Piemonte

Bric Brusata
1712m

Tetti Mecci

Monte Garbella
2306m

Bec
Matlas
2148m

Gias Piamian
1635m

ITALY

Riserva
Bianca

Monte Colombo
2261m

Limonetto
1294m

Ciabot
di Pedu

Monte Ciotto Mien
2378m

Lago degli Alberghi
2032m

1765m

Passo di
Ciotto Mien
2274m

Monte del Frisson

N

Rocca della Bastera
2617m

Cime de Salante
2176m

0   1   2
km

2755m

Monte
Becco Rosso
2126m

FRANCE

provided cable handrail adds confidence, to reach **Passo di Ciotto Mien** (2274m).

Cross the pass ahead and descend among rock and scree initially. This soon gives way to pasture as the path weaves left and right to avoid rocky outcrops. Keep ahead past two side paths joining from the right and continue to meet a track end. Take the track downhill, past **Ciabot di Pedu** (1670m), and continue atop a small ridge. At the lower end as the track divides and becomes tarmac, keep right here and descend through switchbacks to a path left (signposted for Hotel Edelweiss) into **Limonetto** (1294m). As you descend to the main road the tourist information office is on the left, with public WC and free wifi.

FACILITIES INFORMATION FOR STAGE 48

Accommodation

Posto Tappa Arrucador Limonetto, double and twin rooms wifi, Via Maestra, 16, 12015 Limonetto, (CN), +39 348 290 2263

B&B L'Abric, double and twin rooms wifi, Via Maestra, 16, 12015 Limonetto, (CN), +39 348 290 2263

Bragard Hotel, double and twin rooms, wifi, Casali Bragard, 1, 12015 Limone Piemonte, (CN), +39 389 095 2405

Albergo Edelweiss, double and twin rooms, wifi, SP20, 10 Frazione Panice Sottana, 12015, Limone Piemonte, (CN), +39 0171 928138

Amenities

Meals and limited snacks available at accommodation providers.

A small mini market and *tabac* is in Limonetto.

Transport

None on route. However, from Limonetto, nearby Limone Piemonte has a railway station linked to Turin through Cuneo. A taxi is currently the only option to get there, unless an accommodation provider is willing to offer a lift.

STAGE 49

Limonetto to Rifugio Garelli

Start	Limonetto (1294m)
Finish	Rifugio Garelli (1970m)
Distance	23.5km
Ascent	1710m
Descent	1030m
Time	9hr 15min

A day big and beautiful in every way, but this warrants an early start. The climb is dealt with early in the day, after which the route traverses lofty ridges with spectacular views past military forts and marmot strongholds. Crossing the French border briefly, long stretches of ridge walking on old military roads soon shrink the distance to Garelli.

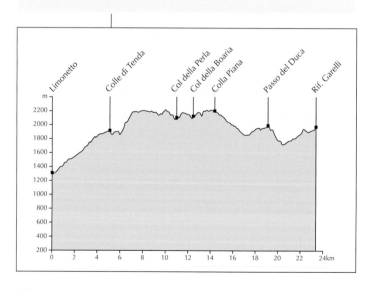

Leaving **Limonetto**, take the steps that lead up through houses, just along from the bar. Emerge onto a track, turn right and proceed uphill. Occasional red/white blazes mark the route. Continue to climb the slope south on grassy switchbacks to reach a broader track. Turn left onto the track, across the **Colle di Tenda** (1871m) and take the track up to the fort itself. Pass behind the main fort building and on up past the front of the higher building, continue across the slope, dropping down again to re-join the lower track and continue to the track junction for Fort Tabourde (on the French side). Leave the track here and take the path west up the nose of the ridge. Near the top keep left emerging onto a higher track marked with France/Italy border posts, passing a viewpoint looking north.

The GTA path now follows the French side of the ridgeline, keep ahead up the switchbacks to the next high point and then keep left (unless you wish to follow the detour out to Fort Pepin). The path skirts behind Cima del Becco (2300m) and drops down to the **Col della Perla** (2080m), climb up the bank opposite rising to pass to the rear of Cima dei Cuni (2259m). Follow the path down to **Col della Boaria** (2100m) and cross the military track here.

Former barracks at Colle di Tenda

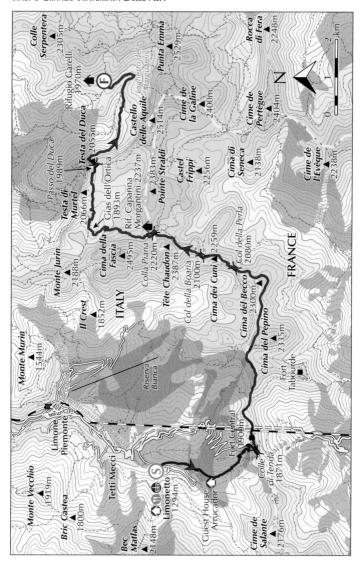

Keep ahead now up the slope where the narrowing path skirts the crags bearing north-east. As you reach a grassy junction marked with a signpost, keep left for the final rise to the border at **Colla Piana** (2220m). A *bivacco* on the left sometimes has a running water source. The descent on the Italian side is a beautiful series of military roads with red/white blazes on rocks to keep you on track. The path circles the basin of Gias dell Ortica (1893m) before climbing again in a broadly westerly direction to reach **Passo del Duca** (1989m). A short way beyond, take a signposted right turn for Rifugio Garelli. Descend sharply to the right from the saddle. The long descent into Valle Margurais divides two thirds of the way down at a fork. The marked path left descends to the *torrente* then climbs gain, the smaller right path stays higher saving some descent and subsequent climb. The paths rejoin near the small **Laghetto del Marguerais**, just below the unexpected small alpine botanical garden. Cross the lake outflow here on rocks, then follow the path northwest to climb the final slope to **Rifugio Garelli** (1970m). Note that on some maps, sections of the route between Col de Tenda and Colla Piana are marked as following the military tracks rather than the ridge paths. Either can be taken, but be aware that occasional vehicles do use the military tracks so care must be taken.

TENDE PASS

The military fortifications so prominent along this section of the trail were built by the Italians around the end of the 19th century to protect the border crossing of the Tende Pass which separates the Maritime and Ligurian Alps. Oddly, the forts now sit on the French side following the border realignment in 1947.

The road tunnel opened in 1882 is 3.2km long and is among the oldest long road tunnels in the world. It was closely followed by a railway tunnel in 1898. However, the pass at Tende far predates this, having had strategic importance right back to the Phoenicians around the mid-12th century BC. It was they who built the earliest road here on the southern most significant alpine pass. After the withdrawal of the Phoenicians, the road which united

Spain, France and Italy for trade, was said to have been kept up and repaired first by the Greeks of Marseille, then by the Romans. The crumbling fortifications that we see today, already disused by the start of the first world war, are in fact relatively modern in comparison to the history of the old road with its 48 hairpin turns.

FACILITIES INFORMATION FOR STAGE 49

Accommodation
Rifugio Garelli, dormitory, Pian Del Lupo, 1, 12013 Chiusa di Pesio, (CN), +39 0171 738078

Amenities
Meals and limited snacks available at accommodation providers.

Transport
None on route.

STAGE 50
Rifugio Garelli to Upega

Start	Rifugio Garelli (1970m)
Finish	Upega (1280m)
Distance	16.25km
Ascent	1130m
Descent	1805m
Time	7hr

An undulating stage that is varied and interesting, going beyond the original southern terminus of the GTA now towards the coast. Despite this, the terrain remains mountainous, and it will be a couple of days before you notice a significant change.

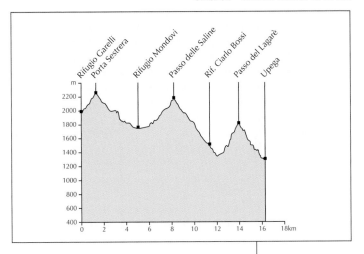

Leaving **Rifugio Garelli**, take the path east, climbing the incline to **Porta Sestrera** (2228m). Just beyond, at the fork, ignore the signposted route to Rifugio Don Barbara, and keep left on the path for Rifugio Mondovi. Dropping down through pasture and wildflowers to a path junction at 2216m, turn left and follow the path above the basin of Lago Biecai (1968m), frequently dry in the summer but providing excellent grazing. The path passes through the narrow stone passageway of **Porta Biecai** (2004m), before dropping into the basin of the Rio Ciappa and skirting around to the right side and over a ridge, until **Rifugio Mondovi** (1761m) comes into view nestled on the plain under the towering crags of Rocche Biecai (2230m).

Continuing from Mondovi, take the gravel track east, keeping right at the track junction to head up the valley. After a hairpin bend in the track look for the signpost indicating a small side path. Turn right here leaving the main track to ascend through meadow towards the pass. The path becomes a little vague here due to cattle tracks, but keep ahead up the ridge in a broadly south then south-west direction to reach **Passo delle Saline** (2174m). Keep straight ahead over the pass. Descending

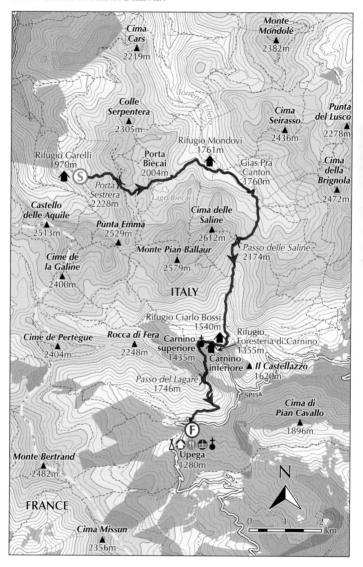

Cima Cars 2219m

Monte Mondolé 2382m

Colle Serpentera 2305m

Torrente Ellero

Cima Seirasso 2436m

Punta del Lusco 2278m

Rifugio Mondovi 1761m

Rifugio Garelli 1970m

S

Porta Biecai 2004m

Gias Pra Canton 1760m

Cima della Brignola 2472m

Porta Sestrera 2228m

Lago Biecai

Castello delle Aquile 2513m

Pùnta Emma 2529m

Cima delle Saline 2612m

Cime de la Galine 2400m

Monte Pian Ballaur 2579m

Passo delle Saline 2174m

ITALY

Cime de Pertègue 2404m

Rocca di Fera 2248m

Rifugio Ciarlo Bossi 1540m

Carnino superiore 1435m

Rifugio Foresteria di Carnino 1355m

Carnino inferiore

Il Castellazzo 1620m

Passo del Lagarè 1746m

SP15A

Cima di Pian Cavallo 1896m

F

Monte Bertrand 2482m

Upega 1280m

N

SP97

FRANCE

Cima Missun 2356m

0   1   2 km

Rifugio Mondovi under the Rocche Biecai 2230m

through pasture, the route again can be vague among cattle tracks. A signpost at Gias delle Saline (1960m) confirms the route. The lower flanks of the Vallone delle Saline become steeper and more rocky as you descend alongside the *torrente*. Shortly after you enter trees, amid the aroma of pine resin, a side trail to the now private **Rifugio Ciarlo Bossi** (1540m) is passed on the right.

At the track junction Tetti delle Donzelle (1540m), you pass the left turn signposted Rifugio Mongoie. Just beyond Viozene, this was the **start/end point of the original classic GTA route**. Most hikers of course now continue to the sea at Ventimiglia, a more satisfying completion.

Shortly after, turn right at a junction signposted 'Upega A5', and continue downhill on a wide track. After a couple of switchbacks look for the smaller path south-west signposted Carnino Inferiore. Take this more direct route, crossing the track again further down. The pretty path through woodland descends into **Carnino Inferiore** alongside the perfectly placed **Foresteria di Carnino** *rifugio* and bar.

Descend to the main road, turn right and walk to the small parking area on the corner where **Carnino Superiore** is signposted through the trees. As you drop onto the road once more, keep ahead across the road and take the path opposite through houses and up steps into the forest behind. At a path junction follow the signposted route left to begin the climb to **Passo del Lagarè** (1746m) and Upega. The descent into **Upega** is simply beautiful and a more gentle gradient than the climb. In Upega, follow the steps down through ancient houses, wooden balconies at unlikely angles weathered and twisted over the years. At the main road, turn right and walk uphill towards the bridge where Locanda d'Upega (1280m) is on the right.

FACILITIES INFORMATION FOR STAGE 50

Accommodation

Rifugio Havis De Giorgio Mondovì, mixed rooms, Località Sella Piscio, 12088 Roccaforte Mondovì, (CN), +39 0174 197 6669

Foresteria di Carnino, mixed rooms, wifi, 18025 Carnino, Province of Cuneo, +39 0174 086108

Locanda d'Upega, double and twin rooms, wifi, Via Provinciale, 14, 12078 Upega, (CN), +39 0174 390401

Amenities

Meals and limited snacks available at accommodation providers.

Transport

None on route.

STAGE 51

Upega to Monesi di Triora

Start	Upega (1280m)
Finish	Monesi di Triora (1374m)
Distance	9km
Ascent	430m
Descent	345m
Time	3hr 45min

A shady section through woodland leads out onto pasture with great views from the *colle*. Across the *colle* a forest track makes easy walking before the descent through Piaggia, where it is impossible to miss the significant damage done by a landslip in 2016 across the valley at the community of Monesi di Mendatica.

From the main road, walk up the street and across the bridge over the river, then turn left to follow the gravel track signposted 'Piaggia 2hr 15min', through the camping site alongside the *torrente*. Keep ahead beyond the campsite and continue on a grassy path. Trail blazes are largely absent here until the path divides at a signpost. Turn left here and cross this tributary stream, returning through trees to join the main *torrente*. While the traditional red/white blazes are absent here, two red dots can be noted on trees on key junctions. A little further on follow the path left across the *torrente* on rocks, and ascend more steeply through trees. A cattle-grazed area beyond makes

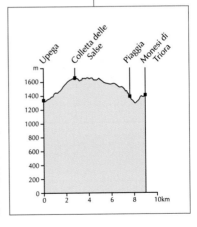

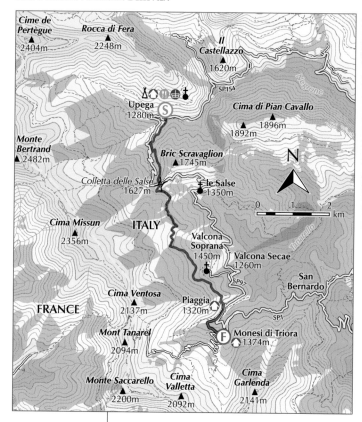

pathfinding difficult but watch for the twin red dots and soon you edge onto the *colle* at **Colletta delle Salse** (1627m).

Cross the *colle* to find the jeep track on the far side bearing right, south-west downhill. Take this track which undulates gently along this wooded hillside.

Just before the buildings at Margheria Binda (1612m), take a path off to the left by small sign indicating to Monesi. Stay on this path which contours around the hamlet of **Valcona Soprana** to reach the grassy knoll at Le

Collette where a prominent cross and statue sit high on the hillside. Turning right here, an ageing signpost indicates the route down from the *colle*, through the ancient village of **Piaggia** (1320m). A series of 'Marguareis Bike' signs guide down steep switchbacks to the road, where you turn right and continue uphill to the bridge across the Torrente Tanarello. Continue uphill on the far side to the broad bus turn-around area where Albergo La Vecchia Partenza, **Monesi di Triora** (1374m) is on your right.

The colle *above* Piaggia

MONESI DI MENDATICA

During the sixties this area was known as the 'Ligurian Switzerland', for its thriving ski resorts that brought jobs and income to these quiet mountain hamlets. Monesi di Mendatica was one of these resorts. While its heyday was long gone, a strong community remained, until November 24 2016, when after several days of heavy rain, a significant landslip occurred that destroyed the provincial road and swept through the centre of the community, sending several houses and other buildings crashing down the mountainside into the *torrente* below. In 2020 a new road was finally opened above the village, but the area remains unstable and looks set to remain a ghost town for the foreseeable future.

FACILITIES INFORMATION FOR STAGE 51

Accommodation
B&B Dolcemente, double rooms, wifi, Via Tanarello, 4, 18025 Piaggia, (CN), +39 346 122 4656

Albergo La Vecchia Partenza, mixed rooms, Via Provinciale, 25, 18010 Monesi di Triora, (IM), +39 331 496 3028

Amenities
Meals and limited snacks available at accommodation providers.

Transport
None on route.

STAGE 52
Monesi di Triora to Colle Melosa

Start	Monesi di Triora (1374m)
Finish	Colle Melosa (1545m)
Distance	20km
Ascent	1275m
Descent	1120m
Time	7hr 45min

A long stage of airy ridges, broad military tracks, and good way marking, it is not difficult to make good time here, but if shorter stages are preferred, or more time wanted for exploring, then the Rifugio la Terza, beyond the statue of the Redentore, underwent a change of ownership and full refurbishment recently and is now a wonderful stay in a unique location.

From **Monesi di Triora**, return across the valley and follow the path up through **Piaggia** (not required of course if you stayed at the delightful B&B Dolcemente in Piaggia), and continue to the balcony below the *colle* where, just beyond a shrine, a signpost at Le Cappellette (1450m), marks the onward track. Turn left here and follow the path uphill through grass and trees passing huts at Case Chizzorane (1545m). Turn left onto a broad military track signposted for Passo di Tanarello. Follow this until it subsequently divides, keep right where the track zigzags steeply upwards and continue to the ridgeline at Passo Basera (2034m).

A short way beyond the *colle*, the path leaves the broad track and follows the ridgeline to **Passo Saccarello** (2150m), then dropping off the ridge to the right. Most however, will stay on the track below the ridge for a short out and back excursion and follow it round to the left to visit the famous statue known as the 'Redentore', and the military fortifications around the summit. If you continued to the statue, a short way further down the ridge you reach the wonderful Rifugio la Terza (2042m).

The **'Redentore'**, or the Redeemer, is an enormous bronze statue of Jesus Christ that was erected on a

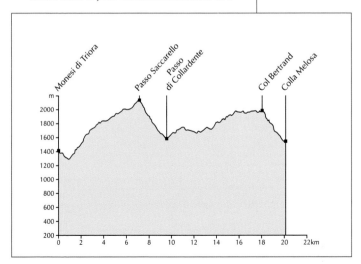

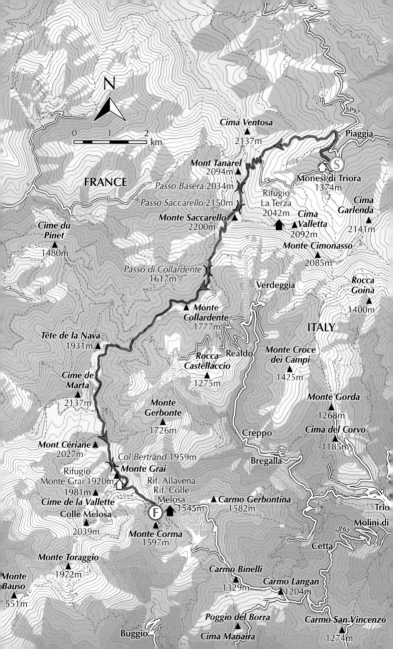

sub peak of Monte Saccarello, at 2164m on the east ridge in 1901. The mountain itself, also known as Mont Saccarel by the French, was Italian until the Paris Peace Treaties of 1947, when the border was realigned, resulting in the sharing of the mountain.

If you left the route to visit the Redentore statue, return by taking the military track that curves north on the way to the true summit, then at the corner of the first switchback, step off the track onto a narrow path and continue just as far as the **Passo Saccarello**, where a signpost guides you left off the ridge and south-west, to descend and traverse the west flank of the mountain into woodland. You are now in France for a short way, and on the path shared by the Alta Via dei Monte Liguri (AVML), signs you will see on much of the route from here to the Mediterranean. Re-join the lower ridge, back on the border now, and follow the marked footpath as it variously touches on or follows the broader military track. This is easy walking and ground is covered quickly while enjoying distant views. Continue beyond **Passo di Collardente** (1617m) and the pass at Bass di Sanson (1694m) then follow the path as it loops north-west for a short stretch to follow the border before dropping south once more, for

Colle Melosa
Ristorante Bar

*Quirky signpost
at Colle Melosa*

The old military barracks at Monte Grai doesn't look very inviting, but it serves as a self-catering hut known as Rifugio Monte Grai, with the keys available at Rifugio Allavena.

a long stretch to **Col Bertrand** (1959m) in front of Monte Grai (2011m). ◄

Just beyond the **Rifugio Monte Grai**, take the path left off the main track leading down a ridgeline then bearing right to join a road end at **Colle Melosa** (1545m).

FACILITIES INFORMATION FOR STAGE 52

Accommodation

Rifugio la Terza, double and family rooms, Località Valletta, 18025 Triora, (IM), +39 0183 754329

Nuovo Rifugio Franca Allavena, dormitory, Colle Melosa, 18037 Pigna, (IM), +39 0184 241155

Colle Melosa Ristorante Bar Rifugio Escursionistico, double and family rooms, wifi, Colle Melosa, 18037 Pigna, (IM), +39 0184 241032

Amenities

Meals and limited snacks available at accommodation providers.

Transport

None on route.

STAGE 53
Colle Melosa to Rifugio Gola di Gouta

Start	Colle Melosa (1545m)
Finish	Rifugio Gola di Gouta (1210m)
Distance	16.25km
Ascent	910m
Descent	1230m
Time	7hr

Glimpses of the Mediterranean in the distance are accompanied by a distinct change in flora now. Dry, dusty paths and hardy scrub on sun-drenched slopes hint at your closing proximity to the coast. This exciting stage initially takes the military path of the Sentiero Degli Alpi for a short way, although an easy alternate is possible. Beyond this the border-hopping continues along a combination of paths and military tracks.

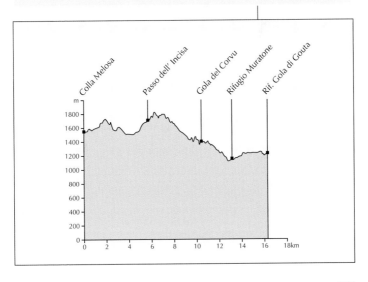

In places the path is cut into sheer cliff

Leave **Colle Melosa** by the gravel track north, passing the path you came in on in the last stage, and continuing around the corner for around 1km to the first sharp hairpin bend. Here you will find a trailhead on the corner, marked as the Fontana Italia. Turn left here along the small, signposted path that clings to the rocks. The narrow path crosses a gully and contours round the hillside with views across to Colle Melosa. You are now on the Senterio Degli Alpini (SDA). In places it is quite exposed, and is often undercut into the cliff. If you don't have a head for heights then one alternative is to return to the Rifugio Monte Grai and follow the ridge path onward to re-join this route at Passo dell'Incisa. A second is to follow the path around the first gully, then take a small path right that climbs to the Passo della Valletta and around the back of Monte Pietravecchia to Passo dell'Incisa

The **Senterio Degli Alpini** was built between 1936 and 1938 to connect the Monte Grai barracks with the defensive line of Monte Pietravecchia-Monte Toraggio. The narrow path was cut into the rock face on extremely steep slopes. In places, the overhanging rock was supported by concrete columns, many have subsequently gone. In 1990 the Ventimiglia section of the CAI, with support from the Province of Imperia, undertook a restoration of the route making it passable for hikers. The first section to Passo dell'Incisa remains open, but the second stage has eroded and at the time of writing had been closed for some years.

Along the way you pass the unlikely but useful water source at Fontana San Martino (1564m). A continual trickle from a crack in the roof of the overhanging cliff, drops 2m into a trough below providing crystal clear cold

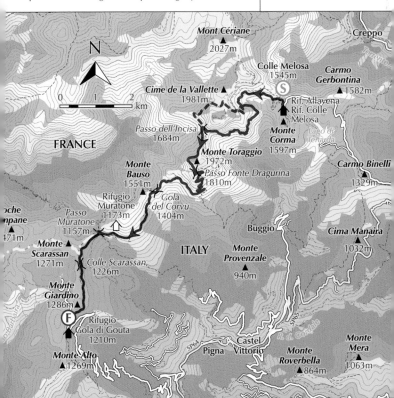

water. Continue until you meet a boulder-strewn gully at the foot of the next pass. This is where the second section of the SDA, recently closed after rockfall, would begin. Instead, take the switchbacks here steeply up to reach the **Passo dell'Incisa** (1684m). Now take the path left along the ridge initially, then traversing right, into France momentarily, below the peak of Monte Toraggio (1972m), before crossing back to the Italian side for a descent through switchbacks, then bearing right below Cima di Logambon (1640m). The path touches on the pass at **Gola del Corvu** (1404m), before bearing left and descending further, where the path becomes broader track once more, then passes the unmanned hut of **Rifugio Muratone** (1173m) to reach the low key **Passo Muratone** (1157m).

Bear left here, remaining on the main track where paths leave to both the left and right. Similarly low key, you'll barely realise you've reached the **Colle Scarassan** (1226m) as you bear left again at a fork, leaving the AVML. Continue along this broad tree-lined track until **Rifugio Gola di Gouta** (1210m) comes into view on your left on the *colle* of Sella di Gouta.

FACILITIES INFORMATION FOR STAGE 53

Accommodation
Rifugio Gola di Gouta, mixed rooms, wifi, Località Sella di Gouta, 18037 Pigna, (IM), +39 329 493 9978

Amenities
Meals and limited snacks available at accommodation provider.

Transport
None on route.

STAGE 54
Rifugio Gola di Gouta to Rifugio Alta Via

Start	Rifugio Gola di Gouta (1210m)
Finish	Rifugio Alta Via (548m)
Distance	16.5km
Ascent	265m
Descent	955m
Time	5hr 45min

This penultimate stage has a real sense of anticipation with the gradient being mostly downhill towards the coast. The stage primarily stays on an old military road known as the Sentiero Balcone, below the ridge, the gentle gradient winding through mixed forest, providing welcome shade interspersed with tantalising glimpses of the coast, old military bunkers and other sites of interest. Water is scarce, however, so carry what you need.

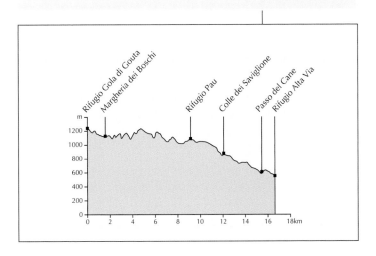

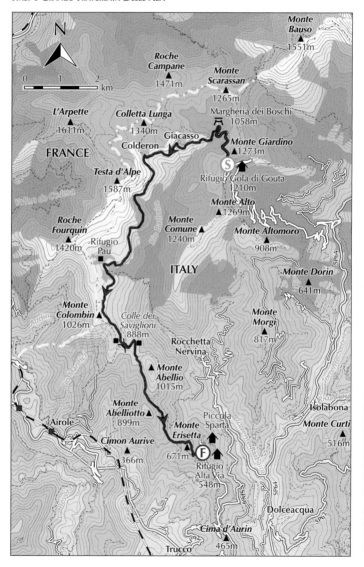

Leave heading north, over the small rise of Sella di Gouta (1213m) and follow the narrow road into the trees. Follow this downhill until the road ends at the picnic and recreation spot of **Margheria dei Boschi** (1058m), then turn left onto a gravel track and head into the trees. After a brief climb keep left at the fork (the right ascends to the ridge path). A little further on an enormous boulder almost blocks the path but can be squeezed past. This dropped from the bank above during heavy rain in 2019, an example of how quickly trail conditions can change.

After the sharp bend and gully crossing pass through the tunnel Galleria Fagania and continue on the old military track, crossing a further spectacular deep gully, which is dry for most of the year. Ignore the subsequent side path to the right and keep ahead. Continue past the Rifugio Pau (1058m – closed at time of writing) and through another tunnel followed by a number of disused military buildings on the right and old horse troughs that

The tunnel Galleria Fagania

281

served the military, now completely dry in this water-less section. The main AVML path re-joins at **Colle dei Saviglione** (888m) and shortly after loops east around conical peak of Monte Abellio (1015m). However, from here you can opt for a smaller more direct path south and passing to the west of Monte Abellio, saving some distance. Re-join the AVML track south of Monte Abellio, at a sign marked Bassa d'Abellio. Continue south-east to a fork where the AVML path leaves the track to the right on the **Passo del Cane** (591m). Keep right here and skirt around the north then east sides of the small top of Monte Erisetta (671m), ignoring side paths. Continue south-east and after a short way look for a small side path left, usu-ally marked with red/white tape and blazes on rocks. This shortcut prevents the need to go ahead and then double-back on the road. Follow this downhill past a water tank and out onto the small road below. Turn left and a few metres up the road find the large sliding gate of **Rifugio Alta Via** on the right.

FACILITIES INFORMATION FOR STAGE 54

Accommodation

Rifugio Alta Via, double and twin rooms, Regione Pozzuolo, 18035 Dolceacqua, (IM), +39 0184 206754

Piccolo Sparta, apartment and rooms, 18035 Dolceacqua Province of Imperia, +39 329 086 4838

Castello Mandrea, Lodging, 18035 Dolceacqua, Province of Imperia, +39 329 008 0683

Agriturismo Terre Bianche, double and twin rooms, Loc. Arcagna snc, 18035 Dolceacqua, (IM), +39 0184 31426

Amenities

Meals and limited snacks available at accommodation providers.

Transport

None on route.

STAGE 55
Rifugio Alta Via to Ventimiglia

Start	Rifugio Alta Via (548m)
Finish	Ventimiglia (0m)
Distance	12.5km
Ascent	160m
Descent	690m
Time	4hr

The final stage remarkably remains high on a ridge all the way to the final cliff descent. Spectacular views of the coast greet you regularly at clearings and corners, and the anticipation of arrival grows. The small ridge line of peaks that you follow diminish to under 500m in height, and the path, undulating across arid plateau for most of this stage, turns at the end for a final steep descent to a road, followed by a bridge and some pavement, then at last, there is nothing more but sea.

As you leave **Rifugio Alta Via**, turn left and walk along the road for a short way to find the rough track on the right leading sharply back on yourself up to the ridge where you can pick up the AVML markers, which you will follow all the way into Ventimiglia now. Once on the

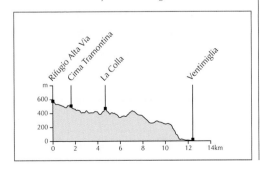

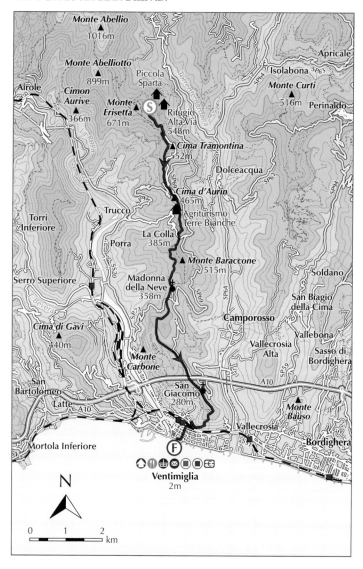

ridge turn left and head south-east, keeping left, uphill at a fork. Prominent ahead of you is the transmission tower on the peak of **Cima Tramontina** (552m). Follow the path to the right of this and continue for a way to reach a small road. Cross and follow the track straight ahead.

Cross a further road at **La Colla** (385m), where the path keeps west of the low peak of Monte Baraccone (515m) and continues across undulating ground to meet the church of **Madonna delle Neve**. Bear right on a smaller path here and across a small road shortly after. Beyond this, cross open ground passing to the right of Monte delle Fontane (473m). Here the ruins of a former military base are scattered around, and you pass close to the organic farm B&B of Le Fontane, should you wish to stay out of town for one more night. At Casa Raimondo keep right on the small path behind the houses. The route now maintains a south-easterly direction, parallel to the small road for a way, past a number of large, gated residential properties. You are now passing directly over the tunnel of the A10 toll road. Reaching the end of the ridge, and the road, turn a corner to the right and then take the small track that leads down the hillside to the left of a property. Follow this down until it joins the end of a small road while enjoying the views left across Ventimiglia and the Mediterranean. At the junction turn left and descend to the railway bridge where on your left is an information board noting this is the western tip of the AVML route. Cross the railway now and turn left into the first street. All that is left is to walk a couple of hundred meters of pavement and you arrive at the Mediterranean Sea in the heart of **Ventimiglia** (2m).

VENTIMIGLIA

Ventimiglia is the ancient capital of the Intimilii, a Liguian tribe around the 1st century AD. The name is derived from Album Intimillium, which became Vintimillium, then Ventimiglia which, on the face of it appears to have a correlation to 'venti miglia' (twenty miles). It is said to be coincidence however that Ventimiglia actually stood almost exactly 20 statute miles from the

French border that stood for almost 500 years between the 14th and the 19th centuries.

Despite being a hugely popular destination for French visitors and tourists on the French Riviera, there is much more to Ventimiglia than a popular tourist destination. Traces of ancient history are here with the caves of Balzi Rossi rich in Palaeolithic remains, including the skeletons of a family of Cro-Magnon people. The 2000-year-old ruins of the old city are around 2km east of the modern town on the plains of Nervia, where parts of the old city walls are still visible. The remains of a 2nd-century Roman theatre have also been uncovered, along with a number of tombs and other artefacts.

Modern Ventimiglia is still a notable destination however, with the Romanesque cathedral dating from the 11th century and the library holding the second-largest collection of 17th-century manuscripts and books in Italy. There is also the Hanbury Botanical Gardens, among the finest in Europe and housing many varieties of tropical and sub-tropical species. Most however, will admittedly come for the Friday street market. An enormously popular event held along the seafront that results in almost complete gridlock in the streets around the front.

The final few metres

The Mediterranean and finish

FACILITIES INFORMATION FOR STAGE 55

Accommodation
Le Fontane B&B, double rooms, wifi, Loc. Montefontane snc, 18033 Camporosso, (IM), +39 328 014 7581

Hotel Calypso, double and family rooms, wifi, Via G. Matteotti, 8A, 18039 Ventimiglia, (IM), +39 0184 351588

Hotel Posta, double and family rooms, wifi, Via Sottoconvento, 15, 18039 Ventimiglia, (IM), +39 0184 351218

Amenities
Ventimiglia is a full-service town with groceries, banks, post office, ATMs and a wide range of restaurants.

Transport
None until Ventimiglia, where the mainline railway station enables a quick connection to the international airport at Nice, taking about 1hr. Take the tramway at Nice from the port to the airport, taking around 30min and costing just €1.50.

APPENDIX A
Italian–English glossary

Italian	English
abisso	chasm, cave
acqua (non) potabile	water (not) suitable for drinking
acqua sorgiva	spring water
affittacamere	B&B
albergo	hotel
alimentari	groceries
alpe	high-altitude summer pasture, farm
autostrada	motorway
bacino artificiale	reservoir
bagni, terme	baths, spa
baita	cabin
balma	rock shelter or cave used by shepherds
bec	rock point
bivacco	unmanned hut for mountaineers
bocca, bocchetta	mountain pass
borgata	hamlet
bosco	wood
bric	isolated rock point
cabinovia	gondola car lift
caire	rocky point
canalone	gully
capanna	hut
carta dei sentieri, carta escursionistica	walking map

Italian	English
casa	house
cascata	waterfall
caserma	military barracks
castello	castle
cava	quarry
chiesa	church
chiot, chiotas	meadow or pasture terrace
cima	peak
colla, colle, colletto	mountain pass
comune	local council district
conca	valley basin, cirque
costa, cresta	ridge
diga	dam
divieto di caccia	no hunting
fermata dell'autobus	bus stop
fonte, sorgente	spring, fountain
foresteria	hostel
frazione	hamlet
funivia	cable-car
galleria	tunnel
gestore	guardian/manager of alpine hut
gias	rudimentary summer shelter for shepherds
giro	tour, circuit
gola	gorge

Italian	English
grangia	alpine farm used in summer
inferiore	lower
ingresso	entrance
invaso	reservoir
lago	lake
lavatoia	washing trough
lose	slate
maira, meira	type of alpine farm for summer use
meublé	B&B
mulattiera	mule track
municipio	town hall
osteria	tavern, wine bar, simple restaurant
panificio, panetteria	bakery
passarella	simple bridge
passo	mountain pass
pasticceria	cake shop
pian, piano	flat, plain, basin
pilone votivo	wayside shrine
ponte	bridge
porta	mountain pass
posto tappa	walkers' hostel
punta	point, summit
ricovero invernale	winter shelter adjoining a refuge
rifugio	mountain hut, usually manned in summer
riserva di caccia	hunting reserve
ristoro	eatery, snack bar
rocca, rocce, rocche	rocky summit

Italian	English
rovine	flow of rubble or soil
seggiovia	chair lift
sella	old-style shepherds' hut for storing cheese, or saddle
sentiero	path
sentiero natura	nature trail
sorgente	source of river, spring
stazione botanica	botanical garden
stazione ferroviaria	railway station
strada	road
superiore	upper
teleferica	mechanised goods cableway
testa	rock point
tetto, tetti	hamlet
torre	tower, mountain
torrente	mountain stream
trattoria	rustic restaurant
trüna	traditional stone hut with vaulted ceiling
uia	mountain
uscita	exit
valle, vallone	valley
vendita formaggi	cheese on sale

APPENDIX B
Useful information

Tourist information

Italian tourist information
www.italia.it

Piedmont regional tourist information
www.visitpiemonte.com/en

Protected parks Piedmont north
www.areeprotetteossola.it

Turin regional tourism
www.turismotorino.org/en

Cuneo regional information
www.visitcuneese.it/en/home

Club Alpino Italiano (CAI)
www.cai.it

Alta Via dei Monti Liguri
www.cailiguria.it/AVML/portale/it/
mare_monti-2.html

Travel

Swiss Travel
www.sbb.ch/en

Trenitalia Rail Travel
www.trenitalia.com/en.html

The Man in Seat 61, rail travel advice
www.seat61.com/train-travel-in-italy.
htm

Maps

Stanfords Map and Travel Bookshop,
London
www.stanfords.co.uk

The Map Shop,
Upton upon Severn
www.themapshop.co.uk

Emergency telephone numbers

Police 112

Ambulance 118

Fire Brigade 115

Forest firefighting service 1515

NOTES

Descending into Alpe Devero (Stage 2)

DOWNLOAD THE ROUTES
IN GPX FORMAT

All the routes in this guide are available for download from:

www.cicerone.co.uk/1040/GPX

as standard format GPX files. You should be able to load them into most online GPX systems and mobile devices, whether GPS or smartphone. You may need to convert the file into your preferred format using a conversion programme such as gpsvisualizer.com or one of the many other such websites and programmes.

When you follow this link, you will be asked for your email address and where you purchased the guidebook, and have the option to subscribe to the Cicerone e-newsletter.

www.cicerone.co.uk

LISTING OF CICERONE GUIDES

BRITISH ISLES CHALLENGES, COLLECTIONS AND ACTIVITIES

Cycling Land's End to John o' Groats
Great Walks on the England Coast Path
The Big Rounds
The Book of the Bivvy
The Book of the Bothy
The Mountains of England & Wales:
  Vol 1 Wales
  Vol 2 England
The National Trails
Walking the End to End Trail

SHORT WALKS SERIES

Short Walks Hadrian's Wall
Short Walks in Arnside and Silverdale
Short Walks in Nidderdale
Short Walks in the Lake District: Windermere Ambleside and Grasmere
Short Walks in the Surrey Hills
Short Walks on the Malvern Hills

SCOTLAND

Ben Nevis and Glen Coe
Cycle Touring in Northern Scotland
Cycling in the Hebrides
Great Mountain Days in Scotland
Mountain Biking in Southern and Central Scotland
Mountain Biking in West and North West Scotland
Not the West Highland Way Scotland
Scotland's Mountain Ridges
Scottish Wild Country Backpacking
Skye's Cuillin Ridge Traverse
The Borders Abbeys Way
The Great Glen Way
The Great Glen Way Map Booklet
The Hebridean Way
The Hebrides
The Isle of Mull
The Isle of Skye
The Skye Trail
The Southern Upland Way
The Speyside Way Map Booklet
The West Highland Way
The West Highland Way Map Booklet
Walking Ben Lawers, Rannoch and Atholl
Walking in the Cairngorms
Walking in the Pentland Hills
Walking in the Scottish Borders
Walking in the Southern Uplands
Walking in Torridon, Fisherfield, Fannichs and An Teallach

Walking Loch Lomond and the Trossachs
Walking on Arran
Walking on Harris and Lewis
Walking on Jura, Islay and Colonsay
Walking on Rum and the Small Isles
Walking on the Orkney and Shetland Isles
Walking on Uist and Barra
Walking the Cape Wrath Trail
Walking the Corbetts:
  Vol 1 South of the Great Glen
  Vol 2 North of the Great Glen
Walking the Galloway Hills
Walking the John o' Groats Trail
Walking the Munros
  Vol 1 – Southern, Central and Western Highlands
  Vol 2 – Northern Highlands and the Cairngorms
Winter Climbs: Ben Nevis and Glen Coe

NORTHERN ENGLAND ROUTES

Cycling the Reivers Route
Cycling the Way of the Roses
Hadrian's Cycleway
Hadrian's Wall Path
Hadrian's Wall Path Map Booklet
The C2C Cycle Route
The Coast to Coast Cycle Route
The Coast to Coast Walk
The Coast to Coast Walk Map Booklet
The Pennine Way
The Pennine Way Map Booklet
Walking the Dales Way
Walking the Dales Way Map Booklet

NORTH-EAST ENGLAND, YORKSHIRE DALES AND PENNINES

Cycling in the Yorkshire Dales
Great Mountain Days in the Pennines
Mountain Biking in the Yorkshire Dales
St Oswald's Way and St Cuthbert's Way
The Cleveland Way and the Yorkshire Wolds Way
The Cleveland Way Map Booklet
The North York Moors
The Reivers Way
Trail and Fell Running in the Yorkshire Dales
Walking in County Durham
Walking in Northumberland
Walking in the North Pennines

Walking in the Yorkshire Dales: North and East
Walking in the Yorkshire Dales: South and West

NORTH-WEST ENGLAND AND THE ISLE OF MAN

Cycling the Pennine Bridleway
Isle of Man Coastal Path
The Lancashire Cycleway
The Lune Valley and Howgills
Walking in Cumbria's Eden Valley
Walking in Lancashire
Walking in the Forest of Bowland and Pendle
Walking on the Isle of Man
Walking on the West Pennine Moors
Walks in Silverdale and Arnside

LAKE DISTRICT

Bikepacking in the Lake District
Cycling in the Lake District
Great Mountain Days in the Lake District
Joss Naylor's Lakes, Meres and Waters of the Lake District
Lake District Winter Climbs
Lake District: High Level and Fell Walks
Lake District: Low Level and Lake Walks
Mountain Biking in the Lake District
Outdoor Adventures with Children – Lake District
Scrambles in the Lake District – North
Scrambles in the Lake District – South
Trail and Fell Running in the Lake District
Walking The Cumbria Way
Walking the Lake District Fells –
  Borrowdale
  Buttermere
  Coniston
  Keswick
  Langdale
  Mardale and the Far East
  Patterdale
  Wasdale
Walking the Tour of the Lake District

DERBYSHIRE, PEAK DISTRICT AND MIDLANDS

Cycling in the Peak District
Dark Peak Walks
Scrambles in the Dark Peak
Walking in Derbyshire
Walking in the Peak District – White Peak East
Walking in the Peak District – White Peak West

For full information on all our guides, books and eBooks,
visit our website:
www.cicerone.co.uk

CICERONE

Trust Cicerone to guide your next adventure, wherever it may be around the world...

Discover guides for hiking, mountain walking, backpacking, trekking, trail running, cycling and mountain biking, ski touring, climbing and scrambling in Britain, Europe and worldwide.

Connect with Cicerone online and find inspiration.

- buy books and ebooks
- articles, advice and trip reports
- podcasts and live events
- GPX files and updates
- regular newsletter

cicerone.co.uk